First Impact

Rod Ellis
Marc Helgesen
Charles Browne
Greta Gorsuch
Jerome Schwab

Development Editors
Anne McGannon
Michael Rost

Longman

For this book,
we recommend:

Published by
Pearson Education Asia Pte. Ltd.
317 Alexandra Road
#04-01 IKEA Building
Singapore 159965

and Associated Companies throughout the world.

© Addison Wesley Longman 1996

This book was developed for Pearson Education Asia by Lateral Communications Ltd., USA.
First published 1996
Reprinted 1999 (twice)

Produced by Pearson Education China Limited, Hong Kong
SWTC/09

Project director: Michael Rost
Developmental editor: Anne McGannon
Project coordinator: Keiko Kimura
Production coordinator: Eric Yau
Text design: Shawver Associates
Cover design: Kotaro Kato, Lori Margulies
Illustrations: Dynamic Duo, Scott Luke, Nikki Middendorf, Amy Wasserman,
                Mark Ziemann, Valerie Randall
Photographs: Don Corning Photograph, The Image Bank, Tony Stone Images
Recording supervisor: David Joslyn

ISBN   Coursebook 962 00 1355 7   Teacher's Manual 962 00 1175 9
        Cassettes   962 00 1157 0   Workbook   962 00 1356 5

The
publisher's
policy is to use
**paper manufactured
from sustainable forests**

Acknowledgements

The authors and editors wish to thank the teachers and students who contributed to this project through interviews, reviews and piloting reports and provided useful comments for revision. In particular, we wish to thank:

Motofumi Aramaki	Mario Ibao	David Progosh
Eleanor Barnes	Michael Keenan	B. Hahn Sang
Michael Barnes	Chae M. Kim	Harumi Sakamoto
Rory Baskin	J. Kim	Michael Sharpe
James Bowers	Chieko Kohno	Don Simmons
David Campbell	Koji Konishi	James Stein
Torkil Christensen	Junko Kurata	Mari Suzuki
Cathy Clark	Hyuk Jin Lee	Alice Svendson
Bill Franke	Hsien-Chin Liou	Laura Swanson
Jeff Frykman	Laura MacGregor	Grant Trew
Peter Gray	Fergus MacKinnon	Charles Tully
William Green	Peter Minter	Carol Vaughan
Su Yup Ha	Ben Mitsuda	Tetsu Watanabe
Hiroko Hagino	Yoko Morimoto	Rebecca Watts
Yoko Hakuta	Hisae Muroi	Robert Weschler
Ken Hartmann	Ryuji Nakayama	Michael Wu
James Heron	Sean O'Brien	Yuli Yeh
Petria Hirabayashi	I. Otomo	Robert Zabrovski
Robert Hutson	David Parkinson	

Special thanks to Lesley Koustaff, Shinsuke Suzuki, Kotaro Kato, Marianne Mitten, and Laurie Margulies for their advice during the project.

The authors would also like to express their personal appreciation to family, friends, and colleagues who assisted them during the project, particularly: Yukari Browne, Gerald Couzens, Carl Dustheimer, Yoko Futami, Yoko Hakuta, Brenda Hayashi, Laitha Manual, Michiko Wako, Dale Griffee, John Gorsuch, Georgia Gorsuch, Keith Avins and Susannah Wakeman.

Thanks to all for your help and support!

Rod Ellis
Marc Helgesen
Charles Browne
Greta Gorsuch   Michael Rost
Jerome Schwab   Anne McGannon

Introduction

Impact is an English coursebook designed to help students develop confidence and skill in using English for communication. The Impact course revolves around the lives of four young professional people: Angela, Gloria, Kazuo and Alex, and their circle of family and friends.

The development of these characters is used as a backdrop for the students to practice information-gathering skills (listening and reading) in context, and as a springboard for the students to express personal opinions about their own lives.

This Coursebook consists of 12 main units and four short Expansion Units. Each main unit is designed for approximately three 50-minute class periods, or two 90-minute periods. Each review unit is designed for approximately two 50-minute periods, or one 90-minute period. A Teacher's Manual, Classroom Cassettes, and Workbook (*First Impact* Workout) accompany the Coursebook and are available separately.

Each of the 12 main units in the Coursebook consists of six parts:
Warm Up
Listening
Conversation Topic
Grammar Awareness
Pair Practice
Read and Respond

WARM UP
This is a short, easy activity that involves all students quickly, introduces them to the theme of the unit and serves as a bridge to the Listening and Conversation Topic sections.

LISTENING
This is a series of three exercises that revolves around a taped conversation. The conversation in this section introduces characters, themes and functions that are carried throughout each unit. There are three types of listening exercises in this section. The first exercise, usually entitled Listening for key words, guides students in identifying the key information and how it is expressed. The second exercise, typically entitled Listening for specific information, guides students in understanding the main information and central purpose of the conversation. The third exercise is an inference question, What do you think?, that encourages students to think about the relationships between the speakers. These three exercises require different but complementary ways of listening.

CONVERSATION TOPIC
This is a guided conversation exercise based on the topic of the Listening extract. This section helps students develop colloquial vocabulary, conversation patterns and strategies for talking about different personal topics. The section consists of two main stages: vocabulary activation and model conversations.

The Word Preview section provides a list of 8-10 vocabulary items based on the topic of the preceding Listening section. A short activation exercise encourages students to work with the meaning of the words.

The Conversation Building section presents a conversation pattern that the students can use as they talk about the topic of the unit. As they practice, the students substitute original information into the conversation model "slots."

GRAMMAR AWARENESS

In this section students are required to notice a particular grammar feature in a spoken extract. The first part of this activity is a listening exercise called Understanding. Students identify key information about a topic or a character. The second part of this activity, Noticing, is a listening exercise utilizing the same discourse used in Understanding, but with a different focus. Here students attend to the grammatical form, completing a specific task. The third part of this activity, Try it, allows the students to produce and share personal information utilizing the target form. The aim is to raise their awareness of how the form is used in actual discourse.

PAIR PRACTICE

This is a simple pair activity, with two parts. A pairwork activity is set up first as an information gap task so that students will ask and answer focused questions with a clear communicative goal. Students work in A/B pairs, looking at different pages in the book. (B pages are in the back of the book.) The second part of the activity, Talking about yourself, builds upon the information gap activity and involves a personal exchange of information or ideas.

READ AND RESPOND

This section provides reading and writing practice, using a variety of short extracts. Each reading is accompanied by a short task to help focus students' attention on the main information. After the reading activity, there is a short writing task and an opportunity for students to exchange their ideas.

EXPANSION UNITS

After every three units, there is a short Expansion Unit, consisting of four activities:

Group Activity

This is a structured group activity that builds on the topics and themes of the units in the preceding section, and allows students to use language creatively.

Learning Check

This is a two-part review of grammar and vocabulary. Through listening and reading tasks, students have an opportunity to assess their progress.

Review Game

This is a fluency-oriented game that recycles vocabulary and grammar from the preceding units.

Learning Better

This is an activity designed to raise students' awareness of different learning styles and to allow them an opportunity to think about and plan changes in their own learning styles.

Meet the characters in Impact

Angela Stevens

Kazuo Ito

Gloria Stevens

Alex Sayers

Karen Henson

Jordan Greene

Julie Greene

Bud and Virginia Stevens

Shawn Wu

David Greene

Sue-Hee Kim

Paulo da Silva

1 NEW PEOPLE

- introducing people
- present tense
- relationships and characteristics

Warm Up *Meeting your classmates*

Write one word about yourself on each line.

Ideas

your hometown *your interests*
your job *your favorite place*
your friends

....

....

....

....

Walk around the class. Introduce yourself to other people.

Look at their books. Ask questions about their words.

Example

Hi, I'm Sondra.
Nice to meet you. I'm Paul.

What's this _____?
That's my hometown.

Listening *"Do you want to meet him?"* 📼

Angela Stevens works for a fashion magazine. She's talking to some people at work.

▼1 Listening for key words
Listen to the conversation. Check (✓) the names and the relationship words you hear.

☐ Corey	☐ Steven
✓ Gloria	☐ Stevens
☐ boss	☐ Kato
☐ Mr. Sayers	☐ Kazuo
☐ Alex	☐ works for
☐ sister	☐ works with

▼2 Listening for relationships
Listen again. What are the relationships? Complete the sentences.

_____*Kazuo*_____ is Angela's co-worker. (They work together.)

_____ is Angela's _____ .

_____ is Angela's _____ .

▼3 What do you think?
Would you like to meet Angela? Why?

Conversation Topic *People in my life* 🎞

1 Word preview

Choose five words. Write a name next to each one.
Then write one word about the person.

Example
Mr. Lane   nice

big brother	....	husband or wife	....
big sister	....	boss	....
little brother	....	co-worker	....
little sister	....	roommate	....
friend	....	neighbor	....
boyfriend	....		
girlfriend	....		

2 Conversation building

Practice this conversation with two other students.
Read the conversation out loud.
Change roles and read the conversation again.

Practice again. Use new words from the Word Preview list.
Now try once more. Use your own ideas.

Grammar Awareness *Angela and Gloria*

Here are Angela and Gloria.
Are they different? How?

1 Understanding
Listen to Angela. Which words
describe her? Write A next
to each one. Which words
describe Gloria? Write G
next to each one.

- [A] quiet
- [ ] talkative
- [ ] serious
- [ ] lots of fun
- [ ] hardworking
- [ ] punctual
  (always on time)
- [ ] always late

2 Noticing
Read the sentences. Find the mistakes and correct them.
Then listen to check.

1. Hi! I ^'m^ Angela. That my sister, Gloria.
2. We twins, but Gloria very different from me.
3. I quiet but she talkative.
4. I a bit serious but she lots of fun.
5. I work a lot. I hardworking. Gloria sleeps a lot. She kind of lazy.
6. I always on time - I a punctual person.
7. But Gloria, oh Gloria - she never on time, she always late.
8. When people see me they always say "Hi, Gloria!"
   I say, "I not Gloria. I Angela." It's a real pain!

3 Try it
Think of someone you know well — your brother, sister, friend, etc.
Write one sentence about you and this person.

I.. , but.. .

Now read your sentence
to your partner.

Grammar Corner

I am - I'm	*I am not - I'm not*
She is - She's	*She is not - She isn't, She's not*
We are - We're	*We are not - We aren't, We're not*

 **Pair Practice** *Circle of friends*

Here are some important people in Angela's life.
Who are they? What are they like?

Example

Who is Gloria?
She's Angela's sister.

What's she like?
She's lots of fun.

1 **Ask and answer questions with a partner.**
Fill in the missing information.

Gloria
Angela's sister
lots of fun

Kazuo
....
....

Julie and Jordan
Angela's neighbors
very talkative

Dave
Angela's boyfriend
lots of fun

Alex
....
....

Virginia

Shawn
Angela's friend
kind of serious

Gandalf
Angela's cat
....

2 **Talking about yourself**
Think of five people who are important to you.
Write their names in the boxes.

PARDON?

CONVERSATION COACH

When you don't understand, ask.

Exchange books with a partner.
Ask your partner about the five people.

Read And Respond *Finding a friend*

1 Reading

Look at these personal ads. Which person would you like to meet? Circle the ad.
Underline the words that show what you like about him or her.

411 Personal	Your Ad
I'm an active and energetic guy. I enjoy hiking, sports and motorcycle racing. I love fun and adventure! D.L. Box 216	
I'm a professional woman. I'm a bit quiet. I love pets, poetry and travel. K.H. Box 351	
I'm a college student. Reading, movies and cooking are my favorite ways to relax. I'm rather serious and caring. S.W. Box 215	
I'm hardworking, but I love to go out, talk with friends and do fun things. A.S. Box 350	

2 Try it

Now write a personal ad that describes you.

3 Shared writing

Work in a group of six. Mix up the ads.
Choose one and read it.
Can you find who wrote it?

Ask questions, for example, "Are you energetic?"

Ideas
active, energetic, hardworking, serious, lots of fun, quiet

2 FIRST IMPRESSIONS

- getting information about people
- singular/plural
- occupations and interests

Warm Up *Comparing ideas*

**What is most important <u>to you</u>?
Circle three things.**

my job

my education

my family background

my age

my interests

the money I have

my clothes

the music I like

my lifestyle

other ....

Compare your choices with a partner.

Listening *"Are you having a good time?"* 📼

Alex is at his friend's wedding in Hawaii.
He doesn't know many people. He's trying to meet someone new.

▼1 Listening for key words
Listen. Check (✓) the words and phrases you hear.

☐ Jim's friend   ☐ live here

☐ Jim's boss   ☐ came for the wedding

☐ are you related   ☐ an art director

☐ we're cousins   ☐ a fashion director

☐ very attractive   ☐ make films

▼2 Listening for personal information
Listen again. What do Karen and Alex find out about each other?
Complete the sentences.

Alex lives in ....

Karen lives in ....

Karen and Jim ....

Alex and Jim ....

▼3 What do you think?
Do you think Karen and Alex like each other? How do you know?
(by words?) (by voice?)

Conversation Topic *Occupations*

1 Word preview

Have you ever met* a musician? an actor?
Read the list. Make a check (✓) under "yes" or "no."

*(meet = talk to face to face)

	Yes, I have.	No, I haven't.
an English instructor		
a newspaper reporter		
an office worker		
a salesperson		
a lawyer		
a flight attendant		
a musician		
a waiter/a waitress		
a professional athlete		
an actor		
a film maker		
a photographer		
Write one more:		

2 Conversation building

Practice this conversation with a partner.
Read the conversation out loud.
Change roles and read the conversation again.

Practice again. Use new words from the Word Preview list.
Now try once more. Use your own ideas.

Grammar Awareness *Buying presents*

Karen is at a gift shop. What kind of presents do you think she will buy?

1 Understanding
Listen. Draw lines from the people to the presents.

younger brother

niece

friend Gloria

father

mother

2 Noticing
Read the sentences.
Find the mistakes
and correct them.
Then listen to check.

> 1. I'm buying my brother computer game.
> 2. I'm getting my niece some comic book.
> 3. I'm buying Gloria a chocolate.
> 4. I'm buying my father some silk shirt.
> 5. And my mother... I'm getting her pineapple.

3 Try it
Imagine you are in Hawaii. What presents would you buy for your family?
Write them here.

....

....

Grammar Corner

a shirt	*some present<u>s</u>*
a pineapple	*some shirt<u>s</u>*

🌼😊 **Pair Practice** *Meet the Hensons*

This is Karen's family.
What do they do? What do they like to do?

1 **Ask and answer questions with a partner.**
Fill in the missing information.

Example

What does Karen do?
She's a film maker.

What does she like to do?
She likes to fix old cars.

Who's Lola?
She's Karen's mother.

Karen
job: a film maker
interest: fix old cars

Lola (mother)
job:
interest:

Simon (father)
job: a lawyer
interest: fencing

Jimmy (older brother)
job: an animal trainer
in the circus
interest: watch
horror movies

Kenny
job:
interest:

Alison (sister-in-law)
job:
interest:

Smiley (pet)
job: protects the house
interest: small animals

2 **Talking about yourself**
Draw a picture of your family tree.
Show it to your partner.
Look at your partner's family tree.
Ask two questions about each person.

COULD YOU SAY THAT AGAIN PLEASE?

If you don't understand the first time ask for help.

19

Read And Respond *Photo memories*

▼ Reading

Look at these photos of Alex and Karen. Match the captions with the photos.

1. Here's Alex and me, dancing at Jim's wedding.
2. The waiter took this picture for us on our first date.
3. This is my favorite photo. I love this blouse.
4. Alex and I like to go shopping together on weekends.
5. Wonder woman. Here I am, fixing Alex's car.

▼ Try it

Choose some photos of yourself to bring to class.
Write a caption for each photo on a piece of paper.

▼ Shared writing

Work with a partner. Mix up your photos and captions.
Can your partner find the right caption for each photo?
Now try to match your partner's photos and captions.

3 BUSY TIMES

- describing routine activities
- simple present tense, adverbs of frequency
- daily activity words

Warm Up *Finding things in common*

Work with a partner.
What activities do you <u>both</u> do – always?
usually? sometimes? occasionally? never?

How many similar activities can you find in 5 minutes?

always ....

usually ....

sometimes ....

occasionally ....

never ....

Example
I always drink coffee in the morning.
I do too.

Listening *"Could we meet after that?"*

Shawn Wu is a university student.
She needs to make an appointment with her professor.

▼1 Listening for key words

Listen. Check (✓) the words and phrases you hear.

☐ early

☐ not a good time

☐ teach my morning class

☐ later today

☐ Wednesday

☐ all morning

☐ between 12 and 1

☐ three times a week

☐ never

☐ too busy

☐ after about 3 o'clock

☐ before that

☐ after that

☐ tonight

☐ tomorrow

▼2 Listening for times

Listen again. Is Dr. Brown's schedule correct? Circle T (for true) or F (for false).

Wednesday			
morning teach classes 9-12	**lunch time** go swimming	**afternoon** faculty meeting	**evening** pick up daughter at 5:00
T F	T F	T F	T F

▼3 What do you think?

Do you think Dr. Brown and Shawn are friends? How do you know?

![icon] Conversation Topic *Activities* 📼

▼1 Word preview

How often do you do these things?
Write a symbol next to each activity in the list.

++++ = every day   +++ = almost every day   ++ = about twice a week   + = about once a month   x = never

.... go swimming

.... have lunch with a friend

.... watch TV

.... write letters

.... go to the library

.... call your boyfriend (girlfriend)

.... listen to music

.... cook dinner

.... visit friends

.... have a meeting

.... go shopping

.... go to class

Now write two more activities.
Put a symbol next to each activity.

....

....

▼2 Conversation building

Practice this conversation with a partner.
Read the conversation out loud.
Change roles and read the conversation again.

Practice again. Use new words from the Word Preview list.
Now try once more. Use your own ideas.

Grammar Awareness *Shawn's day*

Shawn is an exchange student at an American
university. What do you think she does every day?

1 Understanding
Read the questions. Then listen to Shawn.
Check (✓) the correct answers.

When does Shawn's first class usually start?
- [ ] 9:00
- [ ] 10:00

Where does she usually buy her lunch?
- [ ] in the cafeteria
- [ ] at the food stands

What does she always do in the afternoon?
- [ ] goes to class
- [ ] studies in the library

What does she often do in the evening?
- [ ] meets friends
- [ ] works at her part-time job

2 Noticing
Write the frequency word in each sentence. Then listen to check.

1. My first class ^*usually* starts at nine. *(usually)*

2. I go straight to my next class or I go to the library. *(sometimes)*

3. At lunch time we buy something to eat from one of the food stands. *(often)*

4. The food is good and cheap. *(always)*

5. I go to my classes. *(always)*

6. In the evening, I get together with some of my friends. *(usually)*

7. We go to a restaurant. *(sometimes)*

8. We go to expensive places. *(never)*

9. We go to concerts or lectures. *(occasionally)*

3 Try it
Write one thing you always do. Write one thing you never do.
Read your sentences to a partner.

....

....

....

Grammar Corner

I <u>always</u> go to my classes on time.
I <u>usually</u> eat lunch outside.
I <u>sometimes</u> go to the library.

🎭 Pair Practice *A busy life*

Here are some other activities that Shawn does.

Example

Does Shawn ever go shopping?
Yes, a lot.

1 Ask and answer questions with a partner. Fill in the missing information.

How often does she go shopping?
Almost every day.

exercise

a lot ....

4 times a week ....

go shopping

a lot ....

almost every day ....

drink tea

....

....

go to a concert

....

....

eat at an expensive restaurant

....

....

vacuum her apartment

....

....

do volunteer work

occasionally ....

a few times a year ....

see a movie

often ....

almost every month ....

OH REALLY?
WHY DO YOU
DO THAT?

2 **Talking about yourself**

How often do you do the activities above?
How about your partner?
Ask each other questions.
Then ask about three new activities.

If you are interested, ask more questions.

Read And Respond *Letter of introduction*

▼1 Reading

Read this letter from one of the authors of this book.
Think of three questions to ask him —
about his job, his family, his travels.

Example
What are your daughters' names?

Your questions:

1. ....

2. ....

3. ....

Dear Student,

I am one of the authors of First Impact. I'd like to tell you about myself.

I live in Philadelphia — that's in the eastern part of the United States, near New York. I'm a professor at Temple University. I usually teach four days a week but sometimes I have special lectures on weekends. Of course, I spend a lot of time talking with my students. I love teaching.

I live with my wife, Takayo, and our baby daughter. I also have two older daughters by my first wife. The younger one is 14 years old. She lives with us. The older one is 19. She lives in London where she goes to college.

I get up early every day to go jogging. I sometimes play tennis in the morning, too. Then I go to work. When I get home at night, I usually play with the baby.

Every year I travel a lot. This year I'll visit England, Japan and South Africa. I always enjoy visiting countries and meeting new people.

I hope you're enjoying studying English!

Yours,
Rod

▼2 Try it

Now write a personal letter introducing
yourself.

Ideas
Where do you live? What do you do?
What are your free time activities?
What are your plans?

▼3 Shared writing

Work in a group of four. Mix up the letters. Choose one and read it.
Underline the information that is most interesting to you.
Now ask the writer three questions about the information.

GROUP ACTIVITY *Find someone who...*

Stand up. Work with a partner. Ask a question. If your partner says NO, ask a different question. If your partner says YES, write your partner's name. Ask the What or How question. Then find a new partner. Use each name only one time.

Find someone who...

1	...has a dog or cat. *Do you have a dog or cat?*	Partner's name	*What's its name?*
2	...has an older brother or sister. *Do you have...*	Partner's name	*What's his/her name?*
3	...always drinks tea in the morning. *Do you always drink...*	Partner's name	*What kind?*
4	...is kind of lazy. *Are you...*	Partner's name	*What do you hate to do?*
5	...likes to cook. *Do you like...*	Partner's name	*What can you make?*
6	...often goes swimming. *Do you often go...*	Partner's name	*How often?*
7	...is talkative. *Are you...*	Partner's name	*What do you like to talk about?*
8	...has a big family. *Do you have...*	Partner's name	*How many people?*
9	...has a friend who is kind of crazy. *Do you have...*	Partner's name	*What is he/she like?*
10	...occasionally goes jogging. *Do you occasionally go...*	Partner's name	*How often?*
11	...wants (or has) an unusual job. *Do you want...*	Partner's name	*What job?*
12	...listens to music almost every day. *Do you listen...*	Partner's name	*What kind?*

LEARNING CHECK

1 **Word review**
Draw a line from each word in A to its opposite in B.

A		B
quiet		lazy
hardworking		selfish
serious		talkative
caring		plain
attractive		fun

Which of these words describe you? Circle them.

2 **Grammar check**
Gloria is phoning a friend. This is what she says. Fill in the missing words.

Yeah, [1] pretty busy these days. I was in my sister's office about a month

ago, and she introduced me to this really great guy – Kazuo Ito. He's a photographer. Well,

we've started going out together. We see each other nearly every evening. We [2]

just eat out somewhere, but we [3] go to a concert or a movie. And you

know what? Every weekend he sends me [4] present. Last week I got

[5] beautiful flowers. Can you imagine that? He's so thoughtful.

Now listen to Gloria. Check the missing words.

Your Score:_____ / 10

REVIEW GAME *Conversation connections*

Work with a partner. Partner A, ask a question.
Partner B, answer the question and write your name on the square.
Partner B, choose another question.
Partner A, answer that question and write your name on the new square.
Try to finish all the questions on the board. Then go back.
Can you remember your partner's answers?

What's your best friend like?	Who's your best friend?	Who's your favorite actor?
Have you ever met a famous actor?	Who's your favorite teacher?	How often do you study English?
How often do you go shopping?	Where do you like to go shopping?	Where do you like to go on the weekend?
When do you feel lazy?	What do you like to do on Sunday?	What do you like to do on the weekend?
Are you talkative or quiet?	Why are you studying English?	Is your best friend talkative or quiet?
What do you like to do in your free time?	What job would you like to do someday?	What job does your father/mother have?
What did you do last weekend?	Have you ever met a famous musician?	What present would you like to get?
Did you receive any presents on your last birthday?	What's your favorite food?	What food do you like to eat on your birthday?
What month is your birthday?	What is your favorite month?	What is your English teacher like?

LEARNING BETTER *Take your English home*

1 Work with a partner. Look at the cartoon.
What are the people doing in each picture? Write your answers.

1. *They're* ....
....
....

2. *They're* ....
He's ....
but she's ....

3. *He's* ....
Her plant ....
....

4. *His plant* ....
Her plant ....
....

What does this cartoon tell you about learning English?

2 Here are some expressions from Units 1 – 3.

- ☐ Are you from around here?
- ☐ Are you having a good time?
- ☐ Could we meet after that?
- ☐ Do you want to meet him?
- ☐ I get up early every day and go jogging.
- ☐ I love to go out.

- ☐ I'm buying my father some silk shirts.
- ☐ I've heard a lot about you.
- ☐ In the evening, I get together with some friends.
- ☐ Nice to meet you.
- ☐ No, about twice a week.

- ☐ Oh, really? Why do you do that?
- ☐ See you then.
- ☐ She likes to fix old cars.
- ☐ She's lots of fun.
- ☐ Would you like to meet Angela?
- ☐ I'm an actor.

Choose 5 expressions from Units 1-3 that you want to "take home" to remember.
Try to use these expressions this week.

3 **Learning better task**
This week, try to use English outside of class. What new expressions did you use?

When I used English	New expressions I used

4 HIGH TECH

- describing locations
- prepositions
- machines

Warm Up *Everyday machines*

Work with a partner.

How many machines have you used already today?

Write as many as you can in five minutes.

Example
A microwave oven.
A coffee maker…

Listening *"I can't find it"*

Jordan is looking for some things. He's asking his sister, Julie, about them.

1 Listening for key words
Listen. Check (✓) the words and phrases you hear.

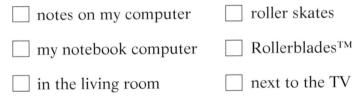

- [ ] notes on my computer
- [ ] my notebook computer
- [ ] in the living room
- [ ] next to the couch
- [ ] on the couch

- [ ] roller skates
- [ ] Rollerblades™
- [ ] next to the TV
- [ ] under the TV

2 Listening for reasons
Listen again. What did Julie borrow from Jordan?

Why did she borrow his things? Write your answers.

3 What do you think?
Do you think Jordan is angry?
Why do you think so?

Conversation Topic *Machines*

1 Word preview

Look at these "high tech" machines. Which do you have? Circle them.
Which do you want? Underline them.

answering machine	fax machine	massage chair
electric toothbrush	pager	TV with remote control
karaoke machine	video game player	
video camera (camcorder)	cordless telephone	Write two more:
computer	laser disk player	
	VCR (video cassette recorder)	
	CD player	

2 Conversation building

Practice this conversation with a partner.
Read the conversation out loud.
Change roles and read the conversation again.

Practice again. Use new words from the Word Preview list.
Now try once more. Use your own ideas.

33

Grammar Awareness *Jordan and the monitor* 📼

Jordan studies in a high-tech classroom.
Do you think he enjoys studying there?

1 ▼ **Understanding**
Listen to Jordan.

Where are Martin and Lily sitting?

Where is the video camera?

Write your answers on the diagram.

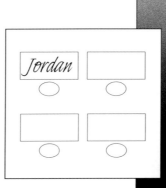

2 ▼ **Noticing**
Read the sentences. Find the mistakes and correct them.
Then listen to check.

1. I was ^ *at* my desk, next Martin.

2. A message came on the small monitor screen front of me.

3. Please do not talk to the student next you.

4. Lily was sitting behind of me.

5. Another message appeared on the monitor in front me.

6. Please do not give anything to the student behind of you.

7. You must smile on class.

8. Tomorrow I'm not going to sit near of that video camera!

3 ▼ **Try it**
Choose three people or things around you. Write three sentences.
Describe where they are.
Use words like: between, next to, on, in front of, behind.

....

....

....

Grammar Corner
in front of the monitor
behind the chair
next to the desk
near the door

Pair Practice *Julie's room*

Julie loves electronic gadgets. Look at her room.

1 **Ask your partner about these four things:**

- a CD player
- a computer
- a cordless phone
- a VCR (video player)

**Write them in the correct place on the picture.
Then answer your partner's questions.**

Example

Does she have a CD player?
Yes.

Where is it?
It's on the bookcase.

Draw these on your picture. Tell your partner where they are.

- a pager
- a massage chair

2 **Talking About Yourself**
Think about your room. What furniture is in it?
Do you have any high-tech gadgets? Where are they?
Describe your room. Your partner will draw it.

HOW DO YOU SAY ___ IN ENGLISH?

If you don't know a word in English, ask.

Read And Respond *I've got to have one!*

1 Reading

Read these catalog advertisements for new products.
Match them with the product they describe.

1. Cellular phone   2. Cyber-helmet   3. Computer game player

4. CD-ROM drive   5. Notebook computer

NOW YOU CAN CALL FROM JUST ABOUT ANYWHERE.

MobilPLUS means mobility
at a price you can afford. Great prices,
plenty of models in stock.

GET MOBILE — NOW!

ARE YOU READY?

If you're ready for the world of
interactive learning, connect the new
Compact XL to your own computer.
It has a tray that lets you pop in disks
just like you do with an audio CD
player. And you won't believe the
world of learning at your fingertips.

The best way to experience virtual reality is to have the right gear to take you there.

*Put this on — it becomes your eyes
and ears — and you're in the future...or
anywhere else you want to be.*

NEW! **500 SERIES!**

It's smaller and lighter than ever
before...the 500 series lets you take your office
home with you. 500 megabytes of memory
and a screen with the best color ever.

---

2 Try it

Now write an advertisement for a new
high-tech product.
Don't write the name of the product.

3 Shared writing

Work in a group of six.

Show your advertisement to your
partners.

Can your partners guess what it is?

Your ad

5 IN TOUCH

- describing actions, talking to friends
- present progressive and present simple
- everyday activities

Warm Up *Right now*

Work with a partner.

How many things are you doing right now?

Make a list.

....

....

....

....

....

....

....

....

Example
We're learning English.
We're talking.

Listening *"Did you get the pictures?"*

Gloria Stevens is on the phone with her dad.
They are talking about some photos of Gloria.

1 Listening for key words
Listen. Which of these verbs ends in ING?
Make a check (✓) next to each one.

☐ do	☐ go	☐ ride
☐ get	☐ sit	☐ stand
☐ look	☐ teach	☐ do
☐ eat	☐ learn	☐ have

2 Listening for responses
Listen again. What does Gloria's dad say about each photo?

restaurant ....

motorcycle ....

Kazuo ....

3 What do you think?
Do you think Gloria likes Kazuo? Why do you think so?

Conversation Topic *What's new?*

1 Word preview

What are you doing these days? Read the list and check (✓) yes or no.
If you check yes, add extra information.

Taking a class	☐ yes ☐ no What kind?	**Working on a new project**	☐ yes ☐ no What kind? ....
Planning a trip	☐ yes ☐ no Where?	**Dating someone new**	☐ yes ☐ no Who? ....
Learning how to do something new	☐ yes ☐ no What?	**Reading a book**	☐ yes ☐ no What kind? ....
Looking for a new place to live	☐ yes ☐ no Where?	**Looking for a job**	☐ yes ☐ no What kind? ....

What else are you doing? Write two more things.

2 Conversation building

Practice this conversation with a partner. Read the conversation out loud.
Change roles and read the conversation again.

Practice again. Use new words from the Word Preview list.
Now try once more. Use your own ideas.

Grammar Awareness *Home for a visit*

Kazuo lives in the U.S. He is visiting his
family in Japan. Who do you think he's talking to?

1 Understanding
Listen to Kazuo.
Circle T (for true) or F (for false).

1. Kazuo is talking to Gloria   **T**   **F**
2. His father is singing love songs.   **T**   **F**
3. His mother is talking about
   the old days.   **T**   **F**
4. His sister is laughing a lot.   **T**   **F**
5. His grandmother is telling stories.   **T**   **F**
6. His brother is playing a game.   **T**   **F**

2 Noticing
**Read Kazuo's letter to Gloria. Fill in the missing verbs. Then listen and check.
Are the verb forms in the conversation the same?**

Dear Gloria,
It was good to speak to you the other day. Every year it's the same old family
reunion. Dad_____ old love songs and _____ about my hair. Mom_____ all
day long and nobody_____ her clean up. Grandma_____ about the old days.
My sister_____ to the stories and _____ — too much! And my little
brother_____ loud rock 'n roll CDs all day long. Still it was nice to be back with
the family.
I miss you a lot. See you soon.
Love,
Kaz

3 Try it
**What are the people in your family probably doing right now? What are some things
they usually do? Write two sentences about what they are doing now. Write two
sentences about what they usually do.**

....

....

**Now write two sentences
about what they always do.**

Grammar Corner	
actions in progress	repeated actions
He is singing love songs.	*He listens to music.*
She is cooking dinner.	*She talks about the old days.*

Pair Practice *New Years holiday*

This is Kazuo's family. Your partner has a similar picture –
with six differences.

1 **Ask your partner where the people are and what they are doing.**
Circle the people and objects that are different.

Example

Where is Kazuo?
He's in the hall.

What's he doing?
He's talking on the phone.

2 **Talking about yourself**
Think of things you do every day. Pantomime the actions.
Your partner will guess. Change roles and continue.

Ideas
dancing, arguing, drinking coffee, eating,
brushing your teeth, putting on make-up,
singing, taking a bath, waiting for a bus.

Example
You're brushing your teeth?
Right.

DID YOU SAY ?

Make sure you understand.

Read And Respond *Thinking of you*

1 Reading

Read Gloria's postcard to Kazuo.

Where is she? Why is she there?

> Dear Kazuo,
> Angela and I are having a great time on our holiday. We're spending a few days in San Diego. Right now I'm lying on a beautiful sunny beach. I'm eating a huge ice cream cone and listening to the CD you gave me — it's great. Angela is swimming in the water and talking to some cute guys. It's perfect. Thinking of you. Come back soon!
> Love,
> Gloria

LOVE

OAKLAND CA 905

Post Card

Kazuo Ito

1-1-2 Shima

Kita-Ku

Sapporo 001 Japan

Dear

Post Card

2 Try it

Imagine you are in an interesting place.

Write a postcard to a good friend. Tell your friend what you are doing right now.

3 Shared writing

Make a group of four. Read each other's postcards. Who is doing the most interesting things?

SPECIAL PLACES

- describing places, making arrangements
- plural nouns
- impressions of places, features of cities

Warm Up *Tell me why*

Think of a place you'd like to visit.
Work with a partner.
Ask where he or she would like to go.
Every time your partner answers, ask, "Why?"
How many times can your partner answer?

Example
Where would you like to go?
To Egypt.

Why?
To see the pyramids.

Why?

Listening *"What's on the morning tour?"* 🔲

Shawn and her friend Sue-Hee are visiting New York City.
They're deciding which places to visit.

1 Listening for key words
Listen. Check (✓) the places you hear.

☐ Central Park   ☐ World Trade Center

☐ Empire State Building   ☐ Wall Street

☐ Trinity Church   ☐ Greenwich Village

☐ Statue of Liberty   ☐ Yankee Stadium

☐ Battery Park

2 Listening for categories
Listen again. Which places are on the morning tour?
Write M next to them. Which are on the afternoon tour?
Write A next to them.

☐ Empire State Building   ☐ World Trade Center

☐ Central Park   ☐ Trinity Church

☐ Battery Park   ☐ Yankee Stadium

☐ Statue of Liberty   ☐ Wall Street

☐ Greenwich Village

3 What do you think?
What do you think Shawn and Sue-Hee will decide to do?

Conversation Topic *Travel*

1 Word preview

Work with a partner. Where can you visit these things?
Write the name of a place.

skyscrapers

Where? ....

castles

Where? ....

open-air markets

Where? ....

small villages

Where? ....

natural attractions (cave, waterfall)

Where? ....

museums

Where? ....

temples or churches

Where? ....

monuments

Where? ....

famous buildings

Where? ....

shopping malls

Where? ....

Write one thing to visit in your city ....

2 Conversation building

Practice this conversation with a partner.
Read the conversation out loud.
Change roles and read the conversation again.

Practice again. Use new words from the Word Preview list.
Now try once more. Use your own ideas.

Grammar Awareness *Philadelphia* 📼

Shawn is an exchange student at a
university in Philadelphia.
What do you know about Philadelphia?

1 Understanding

Listen. Circle the correct information
about Philadelphia.

Philadelphia	
Population:	2,500,000 3,500,000
Location:	between New York and Washington D.C. between New York and Boston
Best to visit in:	summer fall winter spring
Famous sights:	Independence Hall National Museum Old North Church Liberty Bell

2 Noticing

Read the sentences. Find the mistakes and correct them.
Then listen to check.

> I'd like to tell you something about Philadelphia, my new home. Philadelphia is an
> old city of about two and a half million resident. It is on the east coast of the U.S.,
> about 100 mile south of New York and 130 mile north of Washington, D.C. It has
> a similar climate to these city — summer are usually hot and winter are usually
> cold. Spring and fall are the best season. There are lot of famous sights in
> Philadelphia, including Independence Hall and the Liberty Bell. Citizen rang this
> bell when they became independent from Britain over 200 year ago. I really enjoy
> living in Philly!

100 miles = 160km   130 miles = 215 km

3 Try it

Write two sentences about your hometown or your
favorite city.

Grammar Corner

place - places   *city - cities*

....

....

....

Pair Practice *American cities*

Shawn is thinking of visiting other
American cities.

1 **Ask and answer questions with a partner.**
Fill in the missing information.

Example

Where is New Orleans?
It's in the southern part of the U.S.

What's the best time to visit?
Spring.

What's a special thing you can do there?
You can go to the Mardi Gras festival.

What's good to eat there?
Gumbo is a popular dish.

Place	Location	Best season	Special attraction	Best food
New Orleans	southern part of the U.S.	spring	go to the Mardi Gras festival	gumbo (a spicy seafood soup)
Boston				
Seattle	northwestern part of the U.S.	summer	visit the open-air markets	lobster
Denver				
San Antonio	southern part of the U.S.	spring or fall	walk along the river	Tex-Mex chili (spicy stew)
Memphis				
Chicago	midwestern part of the U.S.	spring	visit the Art Institute	pizza

2 **Talking about yourself**
Fill in the information about an interesting city you know.

name of the place: _____

location: _____

special attraction: _____

best food: _____

best season: _____

other information: _____

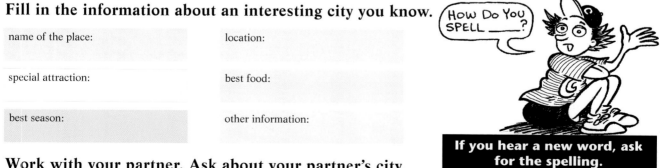

HOW DO YOU SPELL ____?

If you hear a new word, ask for the spelling.

Work with your partner. Ask about your partner's city.

Read And Respond *Special places*

1 Reading

Read the poems* below. Which do you like better?
How do the poems make you feel? Why?

Walking by her side
Should he notice his footsteps
Leave holes in the sand?

Sitting all alone
She watches the setting sun
Finish off the day.

* These are haiku poems, which have a special form.

5 syllables   Sitting all alone   7 syllables   She watches the setting sun   5 syllables   Finish off the day
• • • • •   • • • • • • •   • • • • •

2 Try it

First think of a place that is special to you.
Write a three-line poem about that place.
Write about how the place makes you feel.

3 Shared writing

Make a group of six. Read your poem. Listen to theirs.

GROUP ACTIVITY *Who agrees?*

Complete this questionnaire with your own opinions.

What is...	Your opinion	Who agrees with you?
1 ...a country in Asia you want to visit?		
2 ...the best way to spend an evening alone?		
3 ...an activity or sport you'd like to learn?		
4 ...an electronic item you don't have but wish you did?		
5 ...the most interesting job in the world?		
6 ...an activity or sport you think is stupid, boring, or dangerous?		
7 ...the most interesting city in this country?		
8 ...a personal characteristic (hardworking, talkative, etc.) you think is important?		

Stand up. Work with a partner. Ask a question.
If your partner agrees with you, write your partner's name.
If your partner doesn't agree with you, ask a different question.
Try to write one name on every line. You have 10 minutes.

LEARNING CHECK

▼1 Word review

Label the pictures: pyramid, mall, castle, church, stadium, monument, natural attraction, temple.

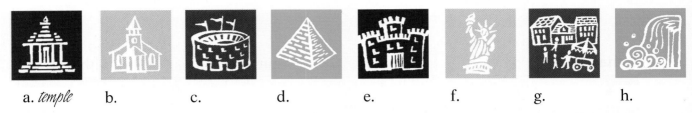

a. *temple*   b.   c.   d.   e.   f.   g.   h.

List the places in the order you would like to visit them.

1st _____   2nd _____   3rd _____   4th _____

5th _____   6th _____   7th _____   8th _____

▼2 Grammar check

Sue-Hee has written a letter to her friend Shawn. Fill in the missing words.

Now listen to Sue-Hee read her letter. Check your answers.

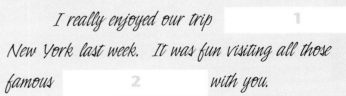

Dear Shawn,

I really enjoyed our trip ___1___ New York last week. It was fun visiting all those famous ___2___ with you.

Did I tell you my brother from Korea was coming? Well, he's here. What a pain! We argue all the time. And he is planning to stay ___3___ the U.S. He ___4___ ___5___ for a job right now and I'm sure he'll get one because he's an electronic whiz kid. He always ___6___ about computers, e-mail, fax machines, and all that stuff all the time. What a bore! What should I do with him?

Yours,

Sue-Hee

Your score: _____ /10

REVIEW GAME *How many can you say?*

Work in groups of five.
Two people are Team A. Two people are Team B. One person is the leader. The leader asks the questions and keeps score. Leader, look at page 104.

Put one book between Team A and Team B.
Listen to the leader's questions. How many items can you say?
You must touch the buzzer each time you answer.

LEARNING BETTER *Think about how you learn vocabulary*

1 **Work with a partner. Look at the pictures.
Match each description with the correct picture.**

1. He put English labels on things in his house.
2. She's testing herself with vocabulary cards.
3. She's relaxing and listening to music while studying new vocabulary.
4. He's drawn a picture next to each vocabulary word.
5. He's making sentences and stories with the new vocabulary words.
6. She's trying to use new words in conversation.

2 **Here are some words and phrases from Units 4-6. Which strategy above could you use to
learn each one? Write the number next to the words and phrases.**

- [ ] answering machine
- [ ] electronic gadgets
- [ ] cellular phone
- [ ] afford
- [ ] at your fingertips
- [ ] caption
- [ ] a new project

- [ ] dating someone
- [ ] that sounds like fun
- [ ] good luck
- [ ] talking about the old days
- [ ] family reunion
- [ ] complain
- [ ] lying on a beautiful beach
- [ ] some cute guys

- [ ] open-air markets
- [ ] monuments
- [ ] climate
- [ ] become independent
- [ ] lobster
- [ ] the setting sun
- [ ] footsteps

3 **Learning better task**
Choose five words you want to learn. Write them in the table.

Words	Strategy	Do you remember?
		YES/NO
		YES/NO
		YES/NO
		YES/NO
		YES/NO

This week try some of the strategies above to learn your five words.
Next week: Do you remember the meaning? Check (✔) yes or no.

DAILY BREAD

- making decisions
- quantity words
- foods, nationalities

Warm Up *Love it, hate it*

**Which foods do you really like? Circle them.
Which do you really dislike? Cross them out (✗).**

sashimi (raw fish)   tomatoes

tofu   green peppers

liver

shellfish

steak

carrots

green tea

coffee

onion rings

fried chicken

pork ribs

bread   raw eggs

Now compare your list with your partner's list.

53

Listening *"How many people are coming?"*

Bud and Virginia Stevens and their daughter Angela are planning a barbecue party.

1 Listening for key words
Listen. Check (✓) the words and phrases you hear.

☐ hamburgers
☐ packages of hamburger meat

☐ bags of those tortilla chips
☐ boxes of those tortilla chips

☐ jars of salsa
☐ cans of salsa

☐ bottles of beer
☐ cases of beer

☐ cans of soda
☐ cases of soda

☐ ice cream cones
☐ carton of ice cream

2 Listening for differences
Listen again. How much food does Bud think they should get?
How much food do they finally decide to get? Fill in the table.

First suggestion		Final decision
......30......	hamburgers	....
....	tortilla chips	....
....	salsa	....
....	beer	....
....	soda	....
....	ice cream	....

3 What do you think?
Do you think they have enough or too much of each thing
(hamburgers, chips, salsa, beer, soda, ice cream)?

⚜ Conversation Topic *Ethnic Dishes* 📼

1 Word preview

Do you know where these dishes are from?
Draw a line from each dish to its nationality.

paella

Kimchee

escargot

sweet and sour pork	Korean
tandoori chicken	Mexican
lasagne	Indian
kimchee	Spanish
escargot	Chinese
paella	Italian
burritos	Japanese
fried chicken	American
sushi	French

Write one more:

Dish: Country:

burritos

2 Conversation building

Practice this conversation with a partner.
Read the conversation out loud.
Change roles and read the conversation again.

Practice again. Use new words from the Word Preview list.
Now try once more. Use your own ideas.

Grammar Awareness *A healthy diet*

Which of these statements are true about you? Check (✓) them.

☐ I eat too much sweet food.   ☐ I don't eat enough fish.
☐ I eat too much red meat.   ☐ I don't eat enough vegetables.
☐ I eat too much salty food.   ☐ I don't eat enough fruit.

1 Understanding

Virginia and Bud are discussing their diet.
Listen. What does she say about each type
of food? Check (✔) the correct column.

Food	too much	too many	enough	not enough
fatty meat				
french fries				
salt				
oil				
sweets				
fat				
sugar				
vegetables				
fish				
fruit				

2 Noticing

Write the quantity words in the correct place in the sentences.
Choose from: *too much, too many, enough.*
Then listen to check.

1. We eat fatty meat.
2. We eat french fries with salt.
3. That's just oil and salt.
4. We eat sweets.
5. Too many sweets means fat and sugar.
6. We don't eat vegetables.
7. We don't eat fish.
8. We do eat fruit.

3 Try it

Write three sentences about your diet.

> **Grammar Corner**
>
> too much salt   enough vegetables
> too many soft drinks   not enough bread

....
....
....

Pair Practice *Food for thought*

What kind of food do you like?

1 **Answer these questions.**
Then ask your partner.
Write your partner's answers.
Do you have the same answers?

Example
What's your favorite kind of ice cream?
Vanilla.

Really? My favorite is chocolate.
Oh. What do you like on pizza?

Question	Your Answer	Your Partner's Answer	Same Or Different
1. What do you like on pizza?			
2. What is your favorite kind of ice cream?			
3. What kind do you really dislike?			
4. What dessert do you like best?			
5. What do you usually have for breakfast?			
6. What kind of potatoes do you like – baked, mashed, or french fried?			
7. What is your favorite spicy food?			
8. What's your favorite soft drink?			
Write one more:			

2 **Talking about yourself**
Work with a partner. Decide the best food for each situation:

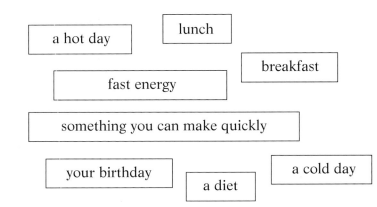

| a hot day | | lunch |

| fast energy | | breakfast |

| something you can make quickly |

| your birthday | | a cold day |

| a diet |

MY FAVORITE KIND OF ICE CREAM IS CHOCOLATE. BUT I SOMETIMES EAT STRAWBERRY.

Conversation is not just question and answer. Add extra information.

Read And Respond *It specializes in...*

1 Reading

Read about the Taj Mahal restaurant.
Would you like to eat there? Why or why not?

NORTH INDIAN CUISINE

The Taj Mahal

The Taj Mahal, located on the corner of Sacramento and Battery streets, is the newest Indian restaurant in town. It specializes in North Indian cooking.

Taj Mahal is authentically Indian. It makes you feel like you're in a Maharajah's palace. However, unlike many other Indian restaurants, this one is very bright inside. You can see what you are eating. It is also spacious and comfortable.

There is an extensive menu, including several tikka (spiced barbecue) dishes and curries to suit every taste. I ordered 'sag ghosh' (mutton cooked in spinach) and 'alu koftas' (spicy potato balls). Both were excellent. A specialty of the Taj is its wide range of Indian sweets. I ordered 'sandesh' (a sweet made out of milk and nuts). It was good but not outstanding.

The quick and efficient service made the meal a real pleasure. The bill was a bit high but the meal was worth it.

Rating: Good   Cost: Moderate

313 Sacramento Street, San Francisco CA 94121 tel: (415) 505-9889 fax: (415) 505-9227

Open for dinner: 6-10 p.m. Monday - Thursday; 5:30 - 10:30 p.m. Friday-Saturday.
Full bar. Reservations and all major credit cards accepted.

---

2 Try it

Now write a review of a restaurant you like.

3 Shared writing

Make a group of four. Read each other's reviews. Choose the restaurant you would like to go to. Say why.

Ideas
Where is it? What is it like inside?
What is the food like? What is the rating?

DIFFERENT WAYS

- explaining rules
- have to, don't have to, should
- cultural rules and customs

Warm Up *It's a rule*

What are some rules you follow at your home, job or school?

Complete the sentences.

We have to ....

....

We should ....

....

We can't ....

....

We're not supposed to ....

....

We shouldn't ....

....

Now work with a partner. Read your rules to each other. Choose one rule you think is a good rule. Choose one rule you think is a bad rule.

Listening *"And one more thing..."*

Julie is on a homestay with a family in Manila.
She is talking with her homestay mother.

1 Listening for key words

Listen. Check (✓) the words and phrases you hear.

- ☐ mention a couple of things
- ☐ tell you a couple of things

- ☐ say goodbye to grandmother
- ☐ say hello to grandmother

- ☐ washed your clothes
- ☐ left your clothes

- ☐ your boyfriend who came to visit
- ☐ your classmate who came to visit

- ☐ it's really not our custom
- ☐ it's our custom

2 Listening for rules

Listen again. What are the three rules at the Aguilars'?
What is the reason for each rule? Fill in the table.

Rule 1: .... Reason: ....

Rule 2: .... Reason: ....

Rule 3: .... Reason: ....

3 What do you think?

What does Julie think of Mrs. Aguilar's rules?

Conversation Topic *Rules*

1 Word preview
Look at the signs. Draw a line from each one to its meaning.

Don't **go in** here.
You can't **smoke** here.
You shouldn't **park** here.
You can't **sit** here.
You're not allowed to **take pictures**.
Don't **touch** this.
You can't **eat** or **drink** anything here.

Draw a sign found in your country.
What does it mean?

2 Conversation building
Practice this conversation with a partner.
Read the conversation out loud.
Change roles and read the conversation again.

Practice again. Use new words from the Word Preview list.
Now try once more. Use your own ideas.

Grammar Awareness *Julie's travel plans*

Julie is joining a group for a tour of Asia before she goes home to the States. Which countries do you think she will visit?

1 Understanding
Listen to Julie talking to the tour organizer.
What's the rule for each action?
Check (✓) your answers.

	have to	don't have to	should
get visas			
go to the embassies			
take a small bag			
put name and tour sticker on bags			
be at the airport by 9 o'clock			
get traveler's checks			
use a credit card			

2 Noticing
Fill in the missing "rule words" *(have to, don't have to, should)* in each sentence. Then listen to check.

have to
1. You ^ get visas for both China and Vietnam.
2. You go to the Chinese and Vietnamese embassies.
3. You take a small bag.
4. You put your name and our tour sticker on your bag.
5. You be at the airport by 9 o'clock.
6. You get traveler's checks.
7. You use a credit card.

3 Try it
What travel rules would you make for visitors to your country? Write three sentences.

....
....
....

Grammar Corner
You have to get a visa.
You should take a small bag.
You don't have to take traveler's checks.

 **Pair Practice** *Exploring Asia*

Student A

Student B, turn to page 106

Here are some customs that Julie noticed on her tour of Asia.

Example

What's an important custom in Japan?
You should take off your shoes before entering a house.

Why?
There are straw mats on the floor.

1 Ask and answer questions with a partner.
Fill in the missing information.

	1. Thailand:	You should leave a little food on your plate. Reason: It shows that you have had enough to eat.
	2. Malaysia:	You should give and receive drinks with .... Why? It shows ....
	3. Hong Kong:	You should point with an open hand, not your finger. Reason: It's more polite.
	4. China:	At dinner, you should .... Why? Your host will .... if you don't.
	5. The Philippines:	Women shouldn't wear shorts in public. Reason: The shorts show too much skin.
	6. Singapore:	You shouldn't make any gestures ....
	7. Indonesia:	You shouldn't eat until the host says to begin. Reason: It shows respect.
	8. Korea:	You shouldn't .... Why not? It isn't ....

2 **Talking about yourself**
Work with a partner.
Write down at least five customs from your country. Do you know the reasons?

WHAT DOES ____ MEAN?

If you need help understanding, ask for more information.

....

....

Do you know any customs from other countries?

Read And Respond *It's taboo*

▼1 Reading

**Taboos are things you should not do. Read about the experiences of five travelers.
Which country are they describing? Number the boxes.**

1. Thailand 4. Taiwan
2. Japan 5. The United Kingdom
3. India

The first time I was there, I had dinner in a nice restaurant. At the end of the meal, I tried to leave a tip for the waitress. It wasn't very much, only 500 yen. But the waitress refused. Then she very politely explained that people do not tip in her country.

When my girlfriend and I were in Chiang Mai, we had to be careful about holding hands or hugging or kissing in public. It's not polite. People consider it too private — people shouldn't do this in front of others, I guess.

The people are very nice, but don't call them "English." Many are not English — they're Welsh, Scot or Irish — from all over the country, really. And they don't like to be called English. Of course, some of the people are English, but it's best to say "British."

Someone once told me never to talk business during a meal. So on my first business trip to Taipei, I was careful to talk about other things: the weather, sports, current events. But you know what everyone else wanted to talk about? Business! I couldn't understand it. Then Mr. Wu explained that talking business while you eat used to be taboo — but now it's OK.

Your country

....
....
....
....
....
....
....
....

I learned about one custom while I was there that was really different. A man should not talk to a woman who is alone in public. That's taboo — it just isn't done. Maybe it has to do with Hindu traditions.

▼2 Try it

What shouldn't people do in your country?

Write about one of your country's taboos.

▼3 Shared writing

**Make a group of four. Read your taboos to the group.
Can you explain why these things are taboo?**

9 STRANGE, BUT TRUE

- describing past experiences
- past tense
- unusual events, reactions

Warm Up *That's very strange*

Work with a partner. Read each experience out loud.

Do you believe it can happen?

- You have a dream and later it really happens.

- You see someone who looks exactly like you.

- You hear noises in the night, but there is no one in the room.

- You think you see a person, but the person died long ago.

- You are thinking about someone and suddenly the person phones you.

- You visit a new place and you feel you have been there before.

Have any of these happened to you?

Tell your partner about it.

Listening *"...and I saw this strange light"* 📼

Alex is telling Karen about a strange thing that happened to him.

1 Listening for key words
Listen. Check (✓) the words and phrases you hear.

☐ happened to me	☐ looked up
☐ went hiking	☐ this strange light
☐ started to get dark	☐ little old man
☐ get back down	☐ I saw his face
☐ started walking	☐ followed him
☐ kept getting darker	☐ knew where he was going
☐ totally lost	☐ tried to thank the man
☐ an owl screeched	☐ disappeared

2 Listening for the story
Listen again. Are these statements true or false? Circle your answers.

1. Alex went hiking yesterday.   **T   F**
2. Alex got lost on the way up the mountain.   **T   F**
3. Alex was scared.   **T   F**
4. Alex was attacked by a wild animal.   **T   F**
5. Alex saw an old man.   **T   F**
6. The man tried to hurt Alex.   **T   F**
7. Alex followed the old man.   **T   F**
8. Alex got home safely.   **T   F**

3 What do you think?
Who was the old man?

☺ Conversation Topic *Experiences*

1 Word preview

Look at these experiences. Imagine they happened to you last night.
Choose a word to describe each experience.

You...	
won a trip to Florida	
were robbed	amazing
got arrested	wonderful
found $100	unbelievable
were almost in an accident	interesting
saw a movie star	surprising
saw Elvis	annoying
lost your wallet	awful
saw a ghost	

2 Conversation building

Practice this conversation with a partner.
Read the conversation out loud.
Change roles and read the conversation again.

Practice again. Use new words from the Word Preview list.
Now try once more. Use your own ideas.

Grammar Awareness *Alex's bad experience* 🔊

Alex is at the airport. A customs officer is asking Alex some questions.
What do you think is in the bag?

1 Understanding
**Read the questions. Then listen to Alex
and the customs officer. Write the answers.**

1. Where did Alex's flight come from?

   ....

2. Why was Alex there?

   ....

3. What did the officer ask Alex to do?

   ....

4. What did the officer find?

   ....

5. Did it belong to Alex?

   ....

6. Who do you think put it there?

   ....

2 Noticing
Write the past tense form of these verbs in the blanks. Then listen to check.

1. pack	....		5. speak	....
2. not put	....		6. want	....
3. keep	....		7. tell	....
4. see	....		8. think	....

3 Try it
Write about a surprising experience. Use at least five different past tense verbs.

Once when I was... ....

....

....

Grammar Corner

Alex arrived at the airport. (arrive)

*The customs officer
found something.   (find)*

Someone put it there.   (put)

Pair Practice *It really happened*

Has your partner ever had a strange or unusual experience?

1 **Ask questions about your partner's experiences. Fill in the chart with your partner's information.**

Have you ever...

Example
Have you ever seen a big fire?
No I haven't / Yes, once.

When did it happen?
About three years ago.

Tell me about it.
Well, about 100 houses burned down.

been questioned by the police?

Yes/No

When:

Extra information:

seen a UFO?

Yes/No

When:

Extra information:

gotten lost while hiking?

Yes/No

When:

Extra information:

seen a big fire?

Yes/No

When:

Extra information:

write another question

met someone famous?

Yes/No

When:

Extra information:

Yes/No

When:

Extra information:

2 **Talking about yourself**
Now think of two more experiences – one that is true and one that is false. Tell your partner the two stories. Can your partner guess which story is true?

WHEN DID IT HAPPEN? WHO WAS WITH YOU? WHERE WERE YOU? WHAT HAPPENED NEXT?

To add extra information, think of WH-questions.

Read And Respond *True stories*

1 Reading

Read these introductions of some true stories.
Think of a title for each story. Write it in the box.
Which story sounds the most interesting? Circle it.

Title:
Andrea was shopping when she saw another woman who looked exactly like her. Who was this woman? Was this her twin? She decided to follow her.

Title:
John was on his way home after visiting his girlfriend. Suddenly he heard footsteps behind him. A small middle-aged man was following him. Who was it? What did the man want?

Title:
Yoko was eight years old. She had a bad dream and woke up in the middle of the night. She went into her parents' bedroom but they were not there. Her elder sister was gone, too. Where were they? Why had they left her alone?

Title:
Matt was playing hide-and-seek with his brother. He hid in a cupboard. When nobody came he tried to get out but the door was stuck. He shouted and shouted but nobody heard him. What would happen to him?

2 Try it

Think of something unusual that has happened to you.
Write an introduction for your own true story.

Ideas
Where were you?
What time was it?
What did you see?
What did you hear?
How did you feel?

Your own true story:
....
....
....
....
....
....
....

3 Shared writing

Exchange introductions with a partner. Read your partner's introduction. Write an ending for the story. Your partner will write an ending for your story.
Now read the whole story. Then ask each other what happened.

GROUP ACTIVITY *Talking Marathon*

Step 1
Choose a topic:

- the best holiday you've had
- the most interesting person you know
- a strange journey you took
- an unusual person you know
- a time that you were very happy

You have one minute to prepare what to say.

Step 2
Now work with a partner. Talk about your topic. Can you talk for two minutes without stopping?

Start like this
I'm going to tell you about…

Partner, listen and check the time.

The turn is over when
- The speaker pauses (stops) for five seconds.
- The speaker says a word that is not English (of course, names of people and places might not be in English).
- The speaker repeats an idea.

Step 3
When the turn is over, the listener asks two questions.

Step 4
Change roles. The first listener becomes the speaker, and talks about his or her topic.

Step 5
When you finish, find a new partner. Talk about your topic again. Try to add new information.

Your best time: _____

LEARNING CHECK

1 Word review
Which word does not belong in each group? Circle it.

pizza (ice cream) hamburger french fries   *cold, sweet*

1 spicy salty happy fatty

2 passport bag embassy traveler's checks

3 Korean American Chinese Japanese

4 amazing wonderful annoying interesting

5 get arrested win a trip lose your wallet see a ghost

Why don't the words belong? Write your reason next to the groups.

2 Grammar check
Julie is talking to her friend Mike. Fill in the missing words.

Julie: I'm enjoying my homestay. Mrs. Aguilar is really nice. But I'm having to learn so

many things. The rules are so different. I _____ some of my own clothes the

other day and she said, "You _____ let the laundry woman do them." And when you

came to see me the other day, she said, "You can't bring a boy to the house. You _____

to meet him somewhere else." That's annoying, but I guess it's part of the culture. I'm

gaining weight too. The food is good, but we eat meat and fried food all the time. I'm

eating too _____ fatty food. I just don't get _____ salad or vegetables.

Mike: Relax. You'll get used to things.

Now listen to Mike and Julie. Check your answers.   **Your score:_____/10**

REVIEW GAME *Speed game*

Work with a partner.
A, choose a topic.
B, choose a question starter. You have 10 seconds to ask a question.
A, you have 10 seconds to answer.
If you can't ask or answer a question in 10 seconds, your partner gets one point.

TOPIC SQUARES

holidays	traveling	foreign food	a bad experience
school rules	boyfriends/ girlfriends	healthy food	home
school	family	customs	a strange experience

10
1   9
2   8
TIME KEEPER
3   7
4   6
5

QUESTION STARTERS

What is your favorite_____?

What_____do you like?

When was the first time you_____?

What_____would you like to have?

What_____would you like to visit?

How many times have you_____?

Who was_____?

Where do you_____?

Score sheet: You:_____ Your partner:_____

LEARNING BETTER *Say it a different way*

1 Look at the cartoon.
In picture 1, the man has a problem. What is the man's problem?
In picture 2, the man solves the problem. How?

picture 1   picture 2

Do you use this technique often?
Does this technique help you in a conversation?
Work with a partner. Try to say these words in a different way.
Say: It's something that…

2 **Learning better task**

Now choose five words or phrases from Units 7-9 that you want to learn.
Write them in the table. Then write another way to say each one.

New word	Another way to say it

10 A GOOD EDUCATION

- talking about plans, expressing opinions
- ways of expressing the future
- academic subjects, opinions

Warm Up *School subjects*

How many school subjects can you list in five minutes? Make a list with your partner.

English

Now circle the subjects you both like.

Cross out (✘) the subjects you both dislike.

Listening *"But that's what I'm interested in"* 🔲

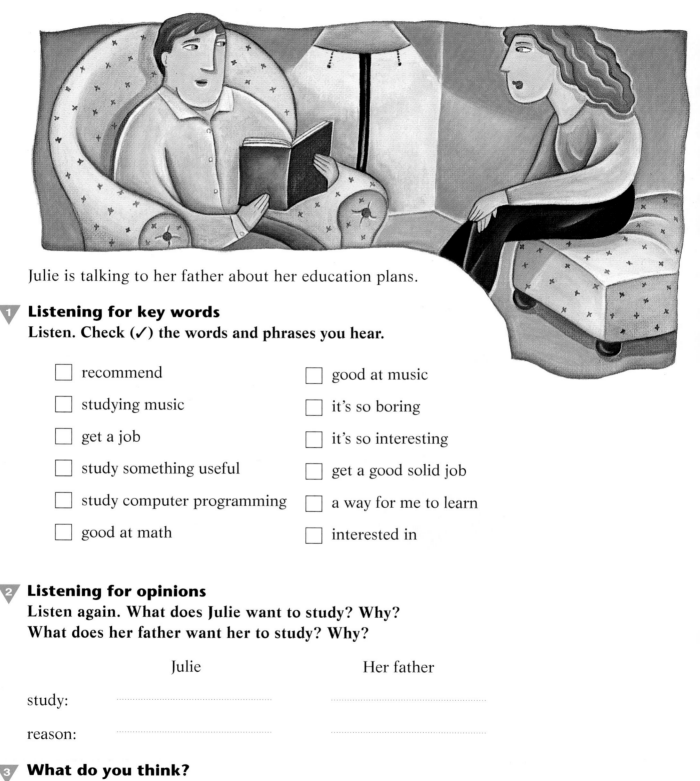

Julie is talking to her father about her education plans.

1 ▸ Listening for key words
Listen. Check (✓) the words and phrases you hear.

☐ recommend   ☐ good at music

☐ studying music   ☐ it's so boring

☐ get a job   ☐ it's so interesting

☐ study something useful   ☐ get a good solid job

☐ study computer programming   ☐ a way for me to learn

☐ good at math   ☐ interested in

2 ▸ Listening for opinions
Listen again. What does Julie want to study? Why?
What does her father want her to study? Why?

	Julie	Her father
study:		
reason:		

3 ▸ What do you think?
Who do you agree with – Julie or her father? Give one reason.

Conversation Topic *Classes*

1 Word preview

Look at these school subjects.
What do you think about them?
Draw a line from each one to your opinion.

Subjects	Opinions
English	exciting
history	fascinating
music	fun
gym	boring
business	interesting
math	dull
art	easy
science	difficult/tough
	simple
	complicated

2 Conversation building

Practice this conversation with a partner.
Read the conversation out loud.
Change roles and read the conversation again.

Practice again. Use new words from the Word Preview list.
Now try once more. Use your own ideas.

Grammar Awareness *Julie's schedule*

Julie is registering for classes at the university.
How many classes do you think she has? What do you think they are?

1 **Understanding**
Listen. Which courses is Julie taking this semester? Circle them.

African Music
American Music
Life Science
English Composition
Music Theory
Basic Spanish
Intermediate Piano

2 **Noticing**
Write the correct form of the verb in each sentence.
Then listen to check.

1. I *registered* this morning. (*register*)
2. I _____ to take an African music course. (*go*)
3. It _____ three times a week. (*meet*)
4. I _____ Intermediate Piano. (*take*)
5. It _____ on Monday. (*meet*)
6. I _____ to take English composition and Basic Spanish. (*go*)
7. I _____ to be really busy. (*go*)

 3 **Try it**
Write three sentences about your plans for this week.

....

....

....

Grammar Corner

I'm going to take American History next semester.

I'm taking Beginning Spanish next semester.

The class meets on Mondays.

Pair Practice *The Entrance Exam game*

Student **A**

Student B, turn to page 108

Play the Entrance Exam game with your partner!

1 **Choose a category and a point value. Tell your partner.**

Your partner will ask you a question. If you answer correctly, you win points!

Your categories:

Movies	The Olympics	World Capitals
10 Points	10 Points	10 Points
20 Points	20 Points	20 Points
30 Points	30 Points	30 Points

Example

I'd like history for 10 points.
OK. The question is, who was the first president of the United States?

Washington?
Yes, that's right. You get 10 points.
or
Lincoln?
No, that's wrong. No points.

Famous People		Music	Numbers
NOBEL PEACE PRIZE	Two South Africans won the Nobel Peace Prize in 1992. Can you name one of them? (Nelson Mandela and F.W. De Klerk)	Can you name all four of the Beatles? (John, Paul, George, Ringo)	How many colors can you see in the rainbow? (Seven)
	Who was the first woman prime minister of India? (Indira Gandhi)	What kind of music is Bob Marley famous for? (reggae)	How many sides are there in a cube? (Six)
	There are four U.S. presidents on the face of Mt. Rushmore. Can you name two? (Washington, Jefferson, Lincoln, Roosevelt)	Who wrote "Bolero"? (Ravel)	What is the name for the number 3.14159? (pi [π]) (three *point* one four...)

Award Ceremony:
Your total: _____ points
Congratulations! You are accepted at Impact University.

2 **Talking about yourself**

Work with a partner. Think of more questions. Ask another pair.

CAN YOU REPEAT THE QUESTION PLEASE?

If you need help understanding, ask.

79

Read And Respond *Lifelong learning*

1 Reading

Lifelong learning centers teach courses to people of all ages.
Read the course catalog. Match the class names with the descriptions.

Stop Now!   Speed Reading   Understanding Your Personality

Men, Women & Relationships   Secret Ways to Health

LIFELONG
LEARNING   *NEW COURSES START NEXT MONTH. SIGN UP NOW!*
CENTER

CLASS NAME:

Yes, we do talk differently. We have different ways of communicating and different needs. In this course, you'll learn a lot about the opposite sex. Most importantly, you'll learn to be more understanding and honest with your partner. Using videos, role play and lectures, we'll work on building stronger relationships.

Thursdays 7 - 9 p.m.

CLASS NAME:

It's the information age. You need to understand information fast. This class will teach you how to organize your thinking as you read. You'll learn how to get the information you need – quickly. Most of all, you'll learn how to build speed.

Wednesdays 7 - 8 p.m.

CLASS NAME:

You know smoking cigarettes is bad and you probably want to quit. You also know that it isn't easy. But you should know: You are in control. In this course, you'll learn the steps that will help you stop. The first step is deciding to do it. Yes, you can do it.

Mondays 7 - 8:30 p.m.

CLASS NAME:

Native American teachers have known natural ways of healing for hundreds of years – plants that make you healthy, natural ways to reduce stress, simple things that make your life better. In this course, you will learn their secrets.

Saturdays 9 a.m. - 2 p.m.

Look at the classes again. Which class would you like to take? Circle it.

2 Try it

What kind of class would you like to take? (or teach!)
Write a description.

....

....

....

Ideas
What will the course teach you?
What makes the course interesting?

3 Shared writing

Work in a group of six. Make a course catalog with your class descriptions.
Show it to another group. Answer questions about your courses.
Ask questions about their courses.

- asking for extra information, describing customs
- count and non-count nouns
- cultural differences

Warm Up *Impressions*

Work with a partner. What are some impressions that other people have of your culture? Try to list 10.

> **Example**
> We're quiet.
> We eat a lot of rice.

....

....

....

....

....

Which ideas are not really true about your culture? Make an ✗ through them.

Listening *"Lots of kids go on dates..."*

Shawn is talking with two friends about dating.
Paulo is from Brazil and Sue-Hee is from Korea.

1 Listening for key words
Listen. Check (✓) the words and phrases you hear.

☐ it's pretty open	☐ dinner at a restaurant
☐ it's pretty strict	☐ to the mountains
☐ about 14 or 15	☐ to the park
☐ about 16 or 17	☐ lots of young people
☐ most of my friends	☐ movies
☐ the right time	☐ in Brazil, too
☐ go on dates	☐ go to the beach
☐ go to coffee shops	☐ the boy or the girl

2 Listening for details
Listen again. When do people in Brazil and Korea start dating?
Where do couples go on dates in Brazil and Korea? Fill in the table.

	Age	Places
Brazil	....	....
Korea	....	....

3 What do you think?
Do you agree with Paulo or Sue-Hee about the best time to start dating?

Conversation Topic *The first time*

1 Word preview
Look at these actions and reactions.
What do you think?

At age 15, is it OK to...	
go on your first date	
move to your own apartment	absolutely not
get your first job	that's a little unusual
get married	I guess that's OK
start drinking alcohol	that's fine
join a sports team	
leave school	
go to your first sleepover party	
stay out past midnight	
get a driver's license	

2 Conversation building
Practice this conversation with a partner.
Read the conversation out loud.
Change roles and read the conversation again.

WHEN DID *YOU* GO ON YOUR *FIRST DATE*?

I *GUESS* WHEN I WAS ABOUT *FIFTEEN*...

REALLY? THAT'S KIND OF *INTERESTING*!

WHY DO YOU THINK SO?

I WENT OUT ON *MY* FIRST DATE WHEN I WAS *EIGHTEEN*!

EIGHTEEN? THAT'S FINE, *TOO*...

Practice again. Use new words from the Word Preview list.
Now try once more. Use your own ideas.

Grammar Awareness *Through a visitor's eyes*

What are some images that people in your country have of the U.S.?

1 Understanding

Sue-Hee and her friend Paulo are talking about American culture.
Listen. What do they say?
Complete the table.

	Paulo	Sue-Hee
food	....	....
sport	....	....
music	....	....
clothing	....	....
name	....	....

2 Noticing

Look at the table below. Which nouns are count and which are non-count? Make an ✘ in the correct column. Then listen to check.

	count nouns (a typical...)	non-count nouns (a typical kind of ...)
food	....	....
sport	....	....
music	....	....
clothing	....	....
name	....	....

3 Try it

Write five sentences about typical things in your country.

food: ....

sport: ....

music: ....

clothing: ....

name: ....

Grammar Corner

count *(a/some)*   **non-count** *(a type of/a kind of)*
a sport/sports   *clothing*
a game/games   *music*

Pair Practice *The culture I know*

What would you tell a person from another country about your culture?

1 **Read the topics and write your answers.
Then answer your partner's questions.**

Example
What do you think is the most important holiday or festival in this country?

New Year's. What do you think?

I think Independence Day is the most important.

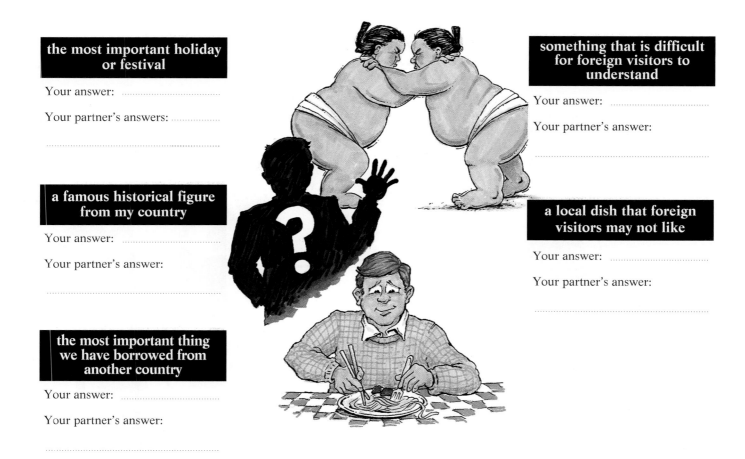

the most important holiday or festival

Your answer: ....

Your partner's answers: ....

....

a famous historical figure from my country

Your answer: ....

Your partner's answer: ....

....

the most important thing we have borrowed from another country

Your answer: ....

Your partner's answer: ....

....

something that is difficult for foreign visitors to understand

Your answer: ....

Your partner's answer: ....

....

a local dish that foreign visitors may not like

Your answer: ....

Your partner's answer: ....

....

2 **Talking about yourself**
A culture capsule is a box of things that will help a foreign visitor understand your culture.

With your partner, make your own capsule.

Choose 10 things to put in the box.

Ideas
*a book, a newspaper,
a kind of food, a gadget,
a game, a music CD,
a piece of clothing*

WHY DO YOU THINK SO?
I THINK...

**Make the conversation your own.
Use your own opinions and ideas.**

Read And Respond *They're everywhere!*

1 Reading
Read these descriptions of current fads. Match them with the correct topic.
Are these fads the same in your country?

1. Bottled water   2. Cellular phones   3. Personal stereos   4. Sweat suits   5.Tattoos

It's a way of saying, "hey, this is me." I know a lot of older people are kind of against them, but all my friends think they're totally great. I know someone who has one on her shoulder, one on her ankle, and one on her hip. It's like art.

You see people wearing them all the time. They're loose and comfortable, so people wear them to the supermarket, around the neighborhood, at home, everywhere. It's not just young kids. Middle-aged men, older women, teenagers, almost everyone wears them. I know they're comfortable, but they're so casual that I only wear them at home.

It's like everyone is in their own private world, wearing little earphones and listening to their own private sounds. They don't hear or see what's going on around them. In a way, they're great, because you never get bored and can always have something to listen to, but I think they prevent human contact.

Everybody's carrying around their own private supply. It just makes you feel more independent. You don't have to spend money on soft drinks and stuff. And it's healthier too because you know exactly what you're putting into your body.

Your Description:
....
....
....
....
....

2 Try it
Write a short description of a fad that's popular in your country.
Don't write a title.

3 Shared writing
Work in a group of six. Read your descriptions out loud. Can your partners guess the trend? What do they think of it?

12 NEXT STEPS

- discussing plans
- questions
- holiday activities

Warm Up *Thank goodness it's Friday (TGIF)*

What are you going to do this weekend? Find at least three things that you and your partner are both going to do.

....

....

....

Now find three things that your partner is going to do that you <u>won't</u> do.

....

....

....

Example
Of course I'm going to study on Saturday.

Really? Me, too.

Listening *"It's Gloria's idea..."*

Kazuo is going on a trip to the Caribbean with Gloria soon.
He's talking to his friend Alex about the trip.

1 Listening for key words
Listen. Check (✓) the words and phrases you hear.

- [ ] taking a trip
- [ ] an island
- [ ] going to do
- [ ] go shopping
- [ ] go with her
- [ ] scuba diving
- [ ] try it

- [ ] rent motorcycles
- [ ] ride around the island
- [ ] do at night
- [ ] go dancing
- [ ] planning this trip
- [ ] my idea
- [ ] Gloria's idea

2 Listening for plans
**Listen again. Is Kazuo going to do these things with Gloria?
Circle yes, maybe or no.**

go shopping	yes	maybe	no
go scuba diving	yes	maybe	no
rent motorcycles	yes	maybe	no
go dancing	yes	maybe	no

3 What do you think?
Why is Kazuo going on this trip?

Conversation Topic *Vacations*

1 Word preview

Which of these things do you like to do on vacation? Circle them.

go shopping	go skiing
go scuba diving	go camping
rent motorcycles	walk around
go dancing	eat at restaurants
visit museums	sit in coffee shops
go swimming	read a lot
lie on the beach	sleep late

2 Conversation building

Practice this conversation with a partner.
Read the conversation out loud.
Change roles and read the conversation again.

Practice again. Use new words from the Word Preview list.
Now try once more. Use your own ideas.

Grammar Awareness *Taking off*

Gloria is packing for her trip. What is she taking with her? Why?

1 Understanding
Angela is asking Gloria about her trip plans.
Listen. Write the question words.

Question Word	Answer
What	I'm packing.
	To the Caribbean.
	Just last week.
	Five days.
	Not much: swimsuit, shorts, warm jacket.
	I need it for skydiving.
	Never.

2 Noticing
Read Angela's questions. Find the mistakes and
correct them. Then listen to check.

1. Where   you're   going?
2. When   you   decided   that?
3. How   long   you   stay?
4. What   you   packing?
5. Why   you   need   that?
6. When   you   learn   how   to   skydive?

3 Try it
Your friend is planning a trip. What do you want to find out? Write five questions.

....

....

....

....

....

Grammar Corner
What are you doing?
Where are you going to stay?
Why do you need that?
When did you buy the tickets?

 **Pair Practice** *Crystal ball*

What is your partner planning to do in the future?

1 **Ask about your partner's plans.**

Then ask one question:
why? when? where? with whom?

Example
Do you think you're going to visit an English – speaking country someday?

Yes, I hope so.

Which country do you want to visit?

Probably Australia.

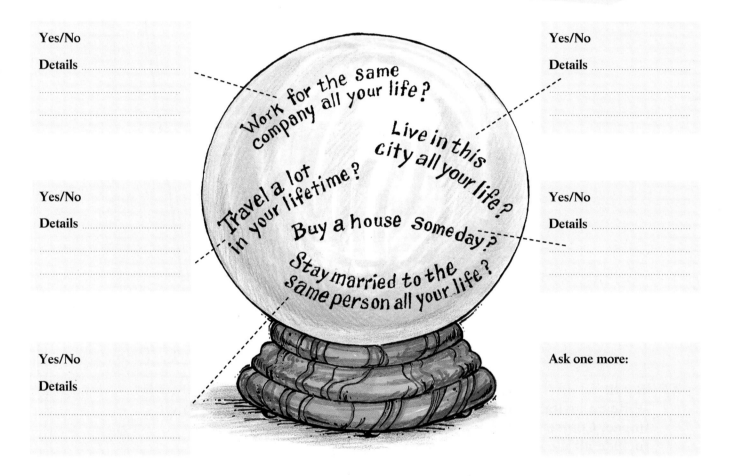

Yes/No

Details

Yes/No

Details

Yes/No

Details

Yes/No

Details

Yes/No

Details

Ask one more:

Work for the same company all your life?

Live in this city all your life?

Travel a lot in your lifetime?

Buy a house someday?

Stay married to the same person all your life?

2 **Talking about yourself**
Work with three other students. Write five sentences about your future. Write each sentence on a different slip of paper.

I'm going to ⎯⎯⎯⎯⎯⎯⎯⎯⎯⎯⎯⎯⎯⎯⎯⎯ .
　　　　　　　 verb 　　　　　　　 *time*

I'LL PROBABLY BUY A HOUSE BECAUSE...

Put all the sentences in a pile and mix them up. Choose one sentence and read it out loud. Guess who wrote it.

Keep the conversation going. Give reasons.

91

Read And Respond *An invitation*

1 Reading
Read this invitation. Who's getting married? Where? When?

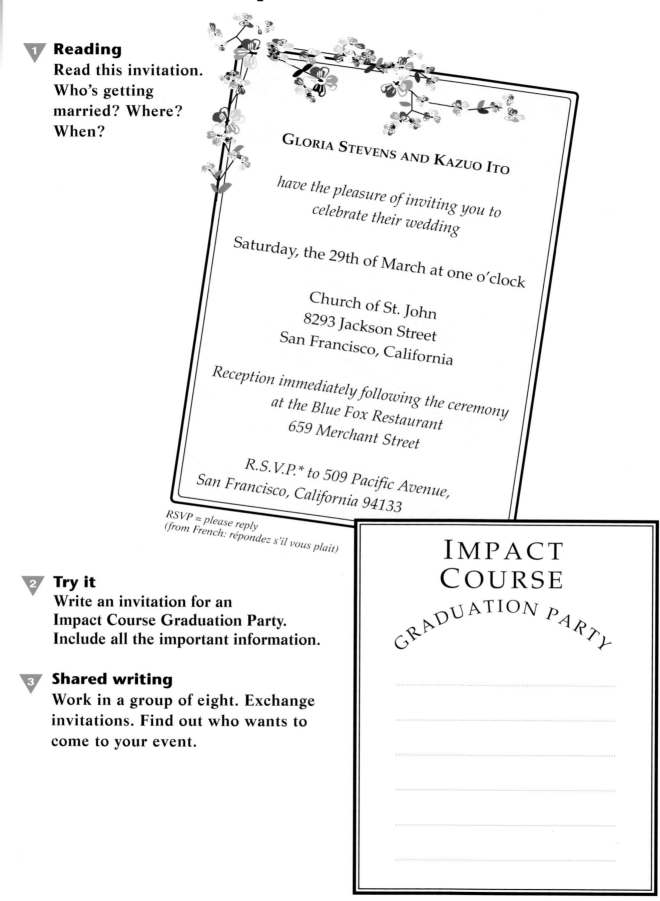

GLORIA STEVENS AND KAZUO ITO

*have the pleasure of inviting you to
celebrate their wedding*

Saturday, the 29th of March at one o'clock

Church of St. John
8293 Jackson Street
San Francisco, California

Reception immediately following the ceremony
at the Blue Fox Restaurant
659 Merchant Street

R.S.V.P.* to 509 Pacific Avenue,
San Francisco, California 94133

*RSVP = please reply
(from French: répondez s'il vous plait)*

IMPACT
COURSE
GRADUATION PARTY

2 Try it
Write an invitation for an
Impact Course Graduation Party.
Include all the important information.

3 Shared writing
Work in a group of eight. Exchange
invitations. Find out who wants to
come to your event.

GROUP ACTIVITY *Who wrote that?*

Step 1:
Fold a piece of paper into six parts.
Copy the sentences.
Finish each sentence.
Then cut the squares apart.

A custom in my country that I think is important is...

A foreign custom I like is...

When I was in high school, I often...

My favorite subject in school was because...

Someday I want to...

In five years I'm going to...

Step 2:
Work in groups of four.
Mix all of your squares together.
One person picks a square. Read it out loud. Guess who wrote it.
The person who guesses correctly picks the next square.

Keep playing.

LEARNING CHECK

1 **Word review**
Use these words to make verb phrases.

verbs	nouns
take	school
go	a motorcycle
get	a trip
join	a team
leave	a class
take	a job
rent	on a date
go	shopping

(take — a trip are connected by a line)

Can you think of one other expression with each of the verbs above?

2 **Grammar check** 📼
Gloria is talking to her sister, Angela. Fill in the missing words.

Well, we _____ to the Caribbean tomorrow. I can't wait. But it wasn't easy to get

Kaz to agree. He kept asking questions. "How long are we _____ ?" "What kind of

_____ do I need to take?" "_____ do we come back?" It almost seemed

like he didn't want to go. Still, he _____ enjoy himself when he gets there.

We always have a lot of fun together.

Now listen to what Gloria says. Check your answers.

Your score:_____/10

REVIEW GAME *Let's talk*

Work in groups of two or three.
Each person needs a space marker.
Put it on the start space.
Close your eyes. Touch the **HOW MANY SPACES** square.
Move that many spaces. Answer the question.
Your answer should have at least five sentences.

H	O	W	M	A	N	Y	S	P	A	C	E	S	?
1	3	2	2	3	1	3	3	2	1	2			
2	1	2	3	1	1	3	2	1	2	3			
1	3	2	3	1	1	2	3	2	1	1			
3	2	1	1	3	2	1	1	2	2	3			
1	3	2	3	1	3	2	1	3	2	2			
2	3	2	1	2	3	3	1	2	3	1			

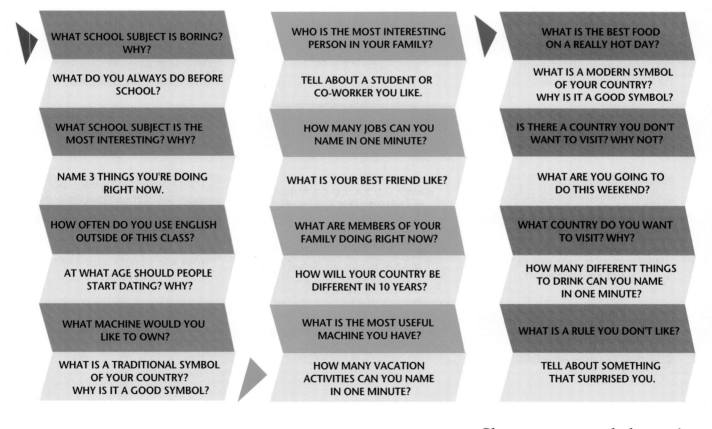

WHAT SCHOOL SUBJECT IS BORING? WHY?

WHAT DO YOU ALWAYS DO BEFORE SCHOOL?

WHAT SCHOOL SUBJECT IS THE MOST INTERESTING? WHY?

NAME 3 THINGS YOU'RE DOING RIGHT NOW.

HOW OFTEN DO YOU USE ENGLISH OUTSIDE OF THIS CLASS?

AT WHAT AGE SHOULD PEOPLE START DATING? WHY?

WHAT MACHINE WOULD YOU LIKE TO OWN?

WHAT IS A TRADITIONAL SYMBOL OF YOUR COUNTRY? WHY IS IT A GOOD SYMBOL?

WHO IS THE MOST INTERESTING PERSON IN YOUR FAMILY?

TELL ABOUT A STUDENT OR CO-WORKER YOU LIKE.

HOW MANY JOBS CAN YOU NAME IN ONE MINUTE?

WHAT IS YOUR BEST FRIEND LIKE?

WHAT ARE MEMBERS OF YOUR FAMILY DOING RIGHT NOW?

HOW WILL YOUR COUNTRY BE DIFFERENT IN 10 YEARS?

WHAT IS THE MOST USEFUL MACHINE YOU HAVE?

HOW MANY VACATION ACTIVITIES CAN YOU NAME IN ONE MINUTE?

WHAT IS THE BEST FOOD ON A REALLY HOT DAY?

WHAT IS A MODERN SYMBOL OF YOUR COUNTRY? WHY IS IT A GOOD SYMBOL?

IS THERE A COUNTRY YOU DON'T WANT TO VISIT? WHY NOT?

WHAT ARE YOU GOING TO DO THIS WEEKEND?

WHAT COUNTRY DO YOU WANT TO VISIT? WHY?

HOW MANY DIFFERENT THINGS TO DRINK CAN YOU NAME IN ONE MINUTE?

WHAT IS A RULE YOU DON'T LIKE?

TELL ABOUT SOMETHING THAT SURPRISED YOU.

Change groups and play again.

Your score:_____

TRIVIA GAME *The Impact Story*

Work with a partner. How many of these questions can you answer?

WHO IS GLORIA'S FATHER?

WHY WAS ALEX STOPPED AT CUSTOMS?

WHAT KIND OF HAIRSTYLE DOES KAZUO HAVE?

WHERE DID KAREN MEET ALEX?

WHAT IS SHAWN'S PROFESSOR'S NAME?

WHICH TWO CHARACTERS VISITED NEW YORK CITY?

WHICH CHARACTER LIVES IN PHILADELPHIA?

WHAT IS ANGELA AND GLORIA'S BROTHER'S NAME?

WHO IS SMILEY? WHAT DOES HE DO?

WHAT DID JULIE DO IN MANILA?

NAME ONE ELECTRONIC THING IN JULIE'S ROOM.

WHAT IS KAZUO'S HOME TOWN?

GLORIA IS ANGELA'S OLDER SISTER. TRUE OR FALSE?

WHO IS JORDAN?

WHAT TWO COUNTRIES WAS JULIE PLANNING TO VISIT?

KAZUO IS ANGELA'S BOSS. TRUE OR FALSE?

WHERE ARE KAZUO AND GLORIA GOING ON THEIR VACATION?

ALEX HAD A STRANGE EXPERIENCE WHEN HE WENT HIKING. WHAT DID HE SEE?

WHAT IS SHAWN'S OCCUPATION?

WHERE DID KAZUO GO DURING HIS NEW YEAR'S HOLIDAY?

WHAT TWO ACTIVITIES ARE KAZUO AND GLORIA GOING TO DO ON THEIR VACATION?

WHY DID JULIE AND HER FATHER HAVE AN ARGUMENT?

WHERE IS SUE-HEE FROM?

HOW ARE GLORIA AND ANGELA DIFFERENT?

WHICH TWO CHARACTERS TALKED ABOUT DATING?

NAME ONE COURSE THAT JULIE STUDIES AT SCHOOL.

Your score:_____

LEARNING BETTER *Use English or you'll lose it!*

This class is almost over. How can you practice English outside of class?

1 Look at these pictures. How are these students using English outside of class?

a. listening to music with English words
b. writing letters to English speaking people
c. writing a notebook or journal in English

d. watching TV or videos in English
e. reading English newspapers and magazines
f. talking to friends in English

Which of these ways do you think are most effective?
Rank them: 1st, 2nd, 3rd, 4th, 5th, 6th.
Work with a partner. See how many more ways you can write.

2 Learning better task
We hope you continue to look for ways to be a better learner after this class is over.
Think about ways of learning and using English outside of class.
Work with a partner. Answer these questions.

What libraries near you have English books?

What English newspapers are available to you?

What are the names of places you go to speak English?

What theaters near you show English language movies?

What video shops near you rent English language videos?

What bookstores sell good books and tapes for learning English?

The best of luck – Rod, Marc, Charlie, Greta, Jerome and your teacher.

Pair Practice *Circle of friends*

Here are some important people in Angela's life.
Who are they? What are they like?

1 **Ask and answer questions with a partner.**
Fill in the missing information.

Example

Who is Gloria?
She's Angela's sister

What's she like?
She's lots of fun

Gloria
Angela's sister
lots of fun

Kazuo
a good friend
really interesting

Julie and Jordan
....
....

Dave
....
....

Alex
Angela's boss
really nice

Virginia
Angela's mom
very nice

Shawn
....
....

Gandalf
....
kind of lazy

2 **Talking about yourself**
Think of five people who are important to you.
Write their names in the boxes.

Exchange books with a partner.
Ask your partner about the five people.

PARDON?

CONVERSATION
COACH

**When you don't
understand, ask.**

Pair Practice *Meet the Hensons*

This is Karen's family.
What do they do? What do they like to do?

Student A, turn to page 19

Example

What does Karen do?
She's a film maker.

What does she like to do?
She likes to fix old cars.

Who's Lola?
She's Karen's mother.

1 **Ask and answer questions with a partner.**
Fill in the missing information.

Karen
job: ....
interest: ....

Lola (mother)
job: a surfing instructor
interest: lift weights

Simon (...............)
job: ....
interest: ....

Jimmy (...............)
job: ....
interest: ....

Kenny (younger brother)
job: he's a high school
    student
interest: cook gourmet food

Alison (sister-in-law)
job: a tattoo artist
interest: go to the opera

Smiley (...............)
job: ....
interest: ....

2 **Talking about yourself**
Draw a picture of your family tree.
Show it to your partner.
Look at your partner's family tree.
Ask two questions about each person.

COULD YOU
SAY THAT
AGAIN PLEASE?

**If you don't understand the
first time ask for help.**

Pair Practice *A busy life*

Here are some other activities that Shawn does.

1 **Ask and answer questions with a partner.
Fill in the missing information.**

Student A, turn to page 25

Example

Does Shawn ever go shopping?
Yes, a lot.

How often does she go shopping?
Almost every day.

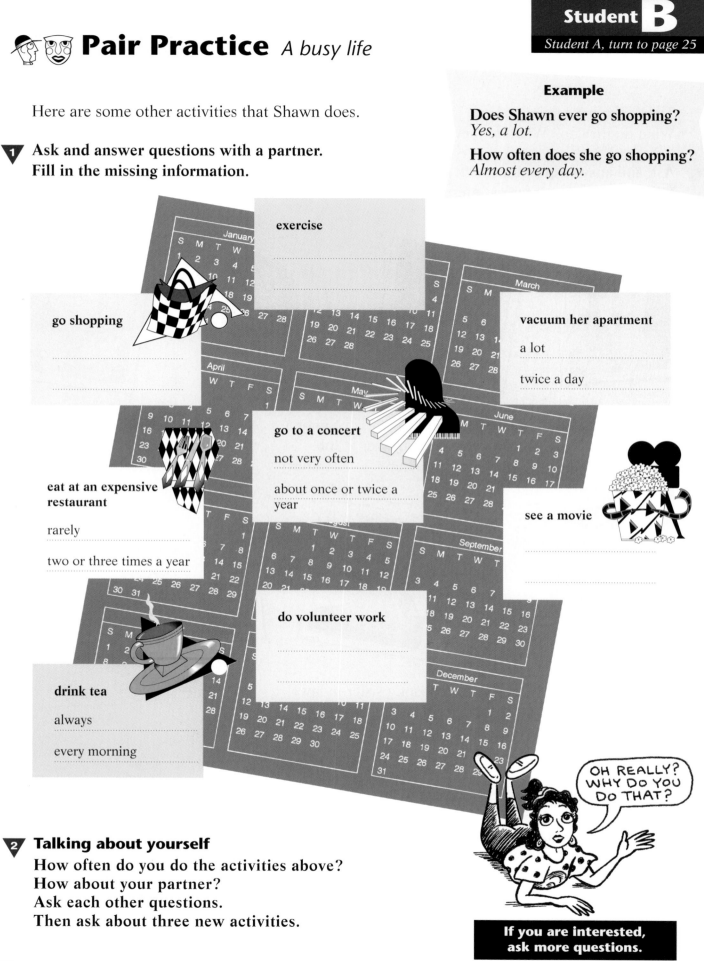

exercise

....

....

go shopping

....

....

vacuum her apartment

a lot

twice a day

go to a concert

not very often

about once or twice a year

see a movie

....

....

eat at an expensive restaurant

rarely

two or three times a year

do volunteer work

....

....

drink tea

always

every morning

OH REALLY? WHY DO YOU DO THAT?

2 **Talking about yourself**
How often do you do the activities above?
How about your partner?
Ask each other questions.
Then ask about three new activities.

If you are interested, ask more questions.

100

🕵️ **Pair Practice** *Julie's room*

Julie loves electronic gadgets. Look at her room.

1 **Ask your partner about these four things:**

- the clock radio
- the video game player
- the karaoke machine
- the electronic keyboard

Write them in the correct place on the picture.
Then answer your partner's questions.

Example

Does she have a CD player?
Yes.

Where is it?
It's on the bookcase.

Draw these on your picture. Tell your partner where they are.

- a camcorder
- a fax machine

2 **Talking about yourself**
Think about your room. What furniture is in it?
Do you have any high-tech gadgets? Where are they?
Describe your room. Your partner will draw it.

HOW DO YOU SAY ___ IN ENGLISH?

If you don't know a word in English, ask.

101

Pair Practice *New Years holiday*

This is Kazuo's family. Your partner has a similar picture – with six differences.

1 **Ask your partner where the people are and what they are doing. Circle the people and objects that are different.**

Example

Where is Kazuo?
He's in the hall..

What's he doing?
He's talking on the phone.

2 **Talking about yourself**
Think of things you do every day. Pantomime the actions.
Your partner will guess. Change roles and continue.

Ideas
dancing, arguing, drinking coffee, eating, brushing your teeth, putting on make-up, singing, taking a bath, waiting for a bus

Example
You're brushing your teeth?
Right.

DID YOU SAY ?

Make sure you understand.

Pair Practice *American cities*

Shawn is thinking of visiting other American cities.

1 **Ask and answer questions with a partner. Fill in the missing information.**

Student A, turn to page 47

Example

Where is New Orleans?
It's in the southern part of the U.S.

What's the best time to visit?
Spring.

What's a special thing you can do there?
You can go to the Mardi Gras festival.

What's good to eat there?
Gumbo is a popular dish.

Place		Location	Best season	Special attraction	Best food
New Orleans		southern part of the U.S.	spring	go to the Mardi Gras festival	gumbo (a spicy seafood soup)
Boston		northeastern part of the U.S.	fall	watch the leaves change color	baked beans
Seattle					
Denver		western part of the U.S.	winter	go skiing in the Rocky mountains	T-bone steak
San Antonio					
Memphis		southern part of the U.S.	anytime	visit Graceland	barbecue ribs
Chicago					

2 **Talking about yourself**

Fill in the information about an interesting city you know.

name of the place:

location:

special attraction:

best food:

best season:

other information:

Work with your partner. Ask about your partner's city.

HOW DO YOU SPELL ____?

If you hear a new word, ask for the spelling.

REVIEW GAME *How many can you say?*

Leader's Page
*Other partcipants,
turn to page 51*

**Ask each question. The teams have one minute to say as many
items as they can. Count (⊮⊦) the answers for each team.**

Answers:

Team A	Team B

Hints

If players don't understand, give an example.

Players must touch the answer buzzer so you can see who said a word first.

Questions:

1. How many kitchen gadgets can you name? (example: a refrigerator)
2. How many countries and capital cities can you name? (example: Seoul, Korea)
3. What actions do you see around you right now? (example: The teacher is walking around the room.)
4. What electronic items have you already used today? (example: a TV)
5. What are popular places for tourists in your country? (example: The Grand Canyon, USA)
6. What are popular places for tourists in your city? (example: The Golden Gate Bridge, San Francisco)
7. What are some famous buildings? (example: The Empire State Building, New York)
8. What do you do with your family during the holidays? (example: We eat dinner together.)
9. Make up your own question.

Pair Practice *Food for thought*

What kind of food do you like?

1. **Answer these questions.**
Then ask your partner.
Write your partner's answers.
Do you have the same answers?

Question	Your Answer	Your Partner's Answer	Same Or Different
1. How do you drink your coffee – black, with cream, or with sugar?			
2. What is your favorite fruit?			
3. What is your favorite foreign food?			
4. What vegetables do you really dislike?			
5. What is one food that you can make well?			
6. How do you like your steak – rare, medium, or well-done?			
7. What is your favorite hot drink?			
Write one more:			

2. **Talking about yourself**
Work with a partner. Decide the best food for each situation:

a hot day

lunch

breakfast

fast energy

something you can make quickly

your birthday

a diet

a cold day

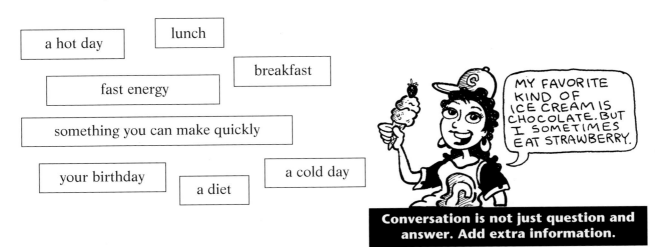

Conversation is not just question and answer. Add extra information.

Here are some customs that Julie noticed on her tour of Asia.

Example

What's an important custom in Japan?
You should take off your shoes before entering a house.

Why?
There are straw mats on the floor.

1 **Ask and answer questions with a partner.**
Fill in the missing information.

	1. Thailand:	You should leave ·· . Why? It shows that you ·································· .
	2. Malaysia:	You should give and receive drinks with two hands. Reason: It shows respect.
	3. Hong Kong:	You should point with ·································· Why? ··
	4. China:	At dinner, you should try at least some of each dish. Reason: Your host will feel bad if you don't.
	5. The Philippines:	Women shouldn't ·································· . Why not? ·································· show ············ .
	6. Singapore:	You shouldn't make any gestures with your fingers. Reason: I don't know. They just don't.
	7. Indonesia:	You shouldn't eat ·································· . Why? It ···
	8. Korea:	You shouldn't eat while walking. Reason: It isn't polite.

2 **Talking about yourself**
Work with a partner.
Write down at least five customs from your country. Do you know the reasons?

WHAT DOES ____ MEAN?

If you need help understanding, ask for more information.

··
··

Do you know any customs from other countries?

106

🎭 Pair Practice *It really happened*

Has your partner ever had a strange or unusual experience?

1 **Ask questions about your partner's experiences. Fill in the chart with your partner's information.**

Have you ever...

Example

Have you ever seen a big fire?
No I haven't / Yes, once.

When did it happen?
About three years ago.

Tell me about it.
Well, about 100 houses burned down.

met someone you know in a faraway place?

Yes/No

When: ....

Extra information: ....
....

been searched at customs?

Yes/No

When: ....

Extra information: ....
....

gotten lost in a big city?

Yes/No

When: ....

Extra information: ....
....

been in an earthquake?

Yes/No

When: ....

Extra information: ....
....

write another question

....
....
....

seen a strange light?

Yes/No

When: ....

Extra information: ....
....

Yes/No

When: ....

Extra information: ....
....

2 **Talking about yourself**
Now think of two more experiences – one that is true and one that is false. Tell your partner the two stories. Can your partner guess which story is true?

WHEN DID IT HAPPEN? WHO WAS WITH YOU? WHERE WERE YOU? WHAT HAPPENED NEXT?

To add extra information, think of WH-questions.

Pair Practice *The Entrance Exam game*

Play the Entrance Exam game with your partner!

1 **Choose a category and a point value. Tell your partner.**

Your partner will ask you a question. If you answer correctly, you win points!

Your categories:

Famous People	Music	Numbers
10 Points	10 Points	10 Points
20 Points	20 Points	20 Points
30 Points	30 Points	30 Points

Example

I'd like history for 10 points.
OK. The question is, who was the first president of the United States?

Washington?
Yes, that's right. You get 10 points.
or
Lincoln?
No, that's wrong. No points.

Movies	The Olympics	World Capitals
In which movies does Sylvester Stallone play a boxer? (the Rocky movies)	How many rings are there in the Olmpic symbol? (five)	What is the capital of Canada? (Ottawa)
Which Steven Spielberg movie is about dinosaurs? (Jurassic Park)	What American won eight gold medals in track and field? (Carl Lewis)	What is the capital of Iraq? (Baghdad)
James Dean was in three movies. Can you name two? (East of Eden, Giant, Rebel Without a Cause)	Where were the first modern Olympics held? (Athens, Greece, in 1896)	What is the capital of Australia? (Canberra)

Award Ceremony:
Your total: _____ points
Congratulations! You are accepted at Impact University.

2 **Talking about yourself**
Work with a partner. Think of more questions. Ask another pair.

CAN YOU REPEAT THE QUESTION PLEASE?

If you need help understanding, ask.

🎭🎭 Pair Practice   *The culture I know*

What would you tell a person from another country about your culture?

1 **Read the topics and write your answers. Then answer your partner's questions.**

Example
What do you think is the most important holiday or festival in this country?

New Year's. What do you think?

I think Independence Day is the most important.

The most important time to give people presents

Your answer: ....

Your partner's answer:

....

A popular person from my country

Your answer: ....

Your partner's answer:

....

The most traditional kind of clothing

Your answer: ....

Your partner's answer:

....

A personality characteristic people respect

Your answer: ....

Your partner's answer:

....

The most important thing other countries have borrowed from us

Your answer: ....

Your partner's answer:

....

A gesture that foreign visitors may not understand

Your answer: ....

Your partner's answer:

....

2 **Talking about yourself**
A culture capsule is a box of things that will help a foreign visitor understand your culture.

With your partner, make your own capsule.

Choose 10 things to put in the box.

Ideas
a book, a newspaper, a kind of food, a gadget, a game, a music CD, a piece of clothing

WHY DO YOU THINK SO? I THINK...

Make the conversation your own. Use your own opinions and ideas.

Pair Practice *Crystal ball*

What is your partner planning to do in the future?

1 **Ask about your partner's plans.**

Then ask one question:
why? when? where? with whom?

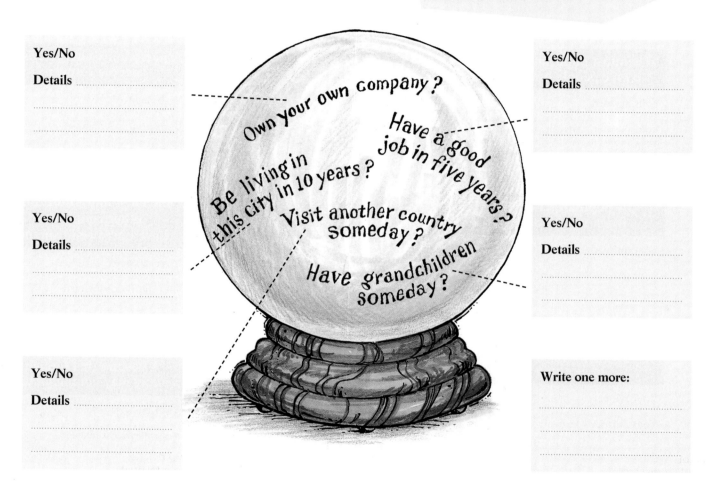

Yes/No

Details

Yes/No

Details

Yes/No

Details

Own your own company?

Be living in this city in 10 years?

Have a good job in five years?

Visit another country someday?

Have grandchildren someday?

Yes/No

Details

Yes/No

Details

Write one more:

2 **Talking about yourself**

Work with three other students. Write five sentences about your future. Write each sentence on a different slip of paper.

I'm going to ....
                verb   *time*

I'LL PROBABLY BUY A HOUSE BECAUSE...

Keep the conversation going. Give reasons.

Put all the sentences in a pile and mix them up. Choose one sentence and read it out loud. Guess who wrote it.

Appendix: Key Words and Expressions

UNIT 1

expressions
Hi, I'm Angela.
Nice to meet you.
This is my boss, Alex.
I've heard a lot about you.
verbs
introduce
meet
do fun things
go out
love
adjectives to describe people
serious
hardworking
nice
lazy
punctual
lots of fun
talkative
quiet
relationship words
big/little brother
big/little sister
friend
boyfriend/girlfriend
boss
co-worker
roommate
neighbor

UNIT 2

expressions
Are you from around here?
What do you do?
What do you like to do?
Are you having a good time?
verbs
work for a fashion magazine
live in San Francisco
buy some presents
get her something
meet someone new
take something home
occupations
actor
English instructor
film maker
flight attendant
lawyer
musician
newspaper reporter
office worker
photographer
professional athlete
salesperson
waiter/waitress

UNIT 3

expressions
Are you free today?
How about tomorrow?
I need to talk to you.
It's not a good time right now.
No, sorry.
See you then.
Would that be a good time?
verbs
teach a class
go swimming
have a meeting
have lunch
visit friends
go to class
write a letter
listen to music
cook dinner
watch TV
get together with friends
time expressions
all morning
between 12 and 1
about 3 o'clock
before 9 o'clock
early
frequency words
always
often
usually
sometimes
occasionally
never
every day
almost every day
about twice a week
about once a month

UNIT 4

expressions
Do you use it a lot?
Have you seen my notebook?
It's in here somewhere.
Please put them back.
There it is.
Where do you keep it?
verbs
borrow my computer
use something
keep something
locations
in the room
under the couch
next to the TV
behind the door
between the desks
in front of the desk
machines and electronic items
answering machine
CD player
remote control
video camera
video game player
cordless telephone
VCR

UNIT 5

expressions
What's new?
Not much.
That sounds like fun.
Good luck.
It was nice to be back home.
verbs
talk on the phone
look at the pictures
eat in the restaurant
learn how to do something
teach someone how to
do some part-time work
take a picture
work on a project
date someone
look for a job
look for a new place to live
complain about something
play CDs
family words
dad (father)
mom (mother)
grandfather
grandmother
nephew
niece
brother-in-law
sister-in-law
everyday things
ice cream cone
beautiful beach
cute guys
family reunion
rock 'n' roll CDs

UNIT 6

expressions
Where did you go on your trip?
What did you do there?
It was wonderful.
When's the best time to visit?
What's good to eat there?
verbs
go skiing
go to a festival
visit a market
walk along the river
places to see
skyscraper
museum
castle
temple
church
open-air market
monument
small village
famous buildings
natural attraction
shopping mall
seasons
spring
summer
fall
winter

UNIT 7

expressions
Let's go out for dinner.
How about Chinese food?
I'll make reservations.
We eat too much salty food.
What's your favorite kind of
   ice cream?

verbs
go out
make reservations
have something to eat

food items
shellfish
tofu
raw fish
pork
chicken
lasagne
salty food
fatty food
red meat
sugar
vegetables
fruit
oil
pizza
ice cream

nationalities
Korean
Mexican
Chinese
Spanish
Indian
Italian
French
American
Japanese

UNIT 8

expressions
Is it OK for me to
   smoke here?
Yeah, that's fine.
By the way
You can't do that here.

verbs
get a visa
take a small bag
put your name on your bag
get travelers checks
use a credit card
be at the airport by 9 o'clock

customs
leave food on your plate
point with your finger
make gestures
show respect
wear shorts
leave a tip

UNIT 9

expressions
You won't believe what
   happened to me.
It scared me.
You're kidding!

verbs
happen
go hiking
get dark
get back
start walking
hear something
win a trip
be robbed
get arrested
lose something
be searched

words to describe feelings
amazing
wonderful
interesting
surprising
surprised
weird
annoying
awful
scared
unbelievable

UNIT 10

expressions
I'm interested in that.
It's so boring.
I'm thinking of studying that.
What classes are you taking?
How do you like them?

verbs
study something useful
get a good job
recommend
plan
register
meet every Friday
be busy

school subjects
English
math
science
history
music
gym
art
computer science
business

words to describe opinions
exciting
fascinating
fun
boring
interesting
dull
easy
tough
simple
complicated

UNIT 11

expressions
Why do you think so?
That's kind of surprising.
That's fine.
It depends.

first experiences
go on your first date
move to your own apartment
get your first job
get married
join a sports team
leave school
stay out past midnight
get a driver's license

culture items
a typical sport
a local dish
a popular person
a traditional kind of clothing
a personality characteristic
a kind of music
a kind of clothing

American culture
pizza
hamburgers
football
baseball
country music
jazz
basketball shoes
baseball hats

UNIT 12

expressions
You're taking a trip, huh?
You always go to such
   interesting places.
Can I go with you?
Definitely.

verbs
pack
fly
leave
decide
stay in a hotel
need
take lessons
go with you
leave tomorrow

vacation activities
go scuba diving
go skydiving
rent motorcycles
go dancing
lie on the beach
go camping
walk around
eat at restaurants
sit in coffee shops
read a lot
sleep late